FINDING FREEDOM

Five Weeks in the Life of Moses

DONNA J. STUNDAHL

WESTBOW®
PRESS
A DIVISION OF THOMAS NELSON
& ZONDERVAN

WestBow Press books may be ordered through booksellers or by contacting:

WestBow Press
A Division of Thomas Nelson & Zondervan
1663 Liberty Drive
Bloomington, IN 47403
www.westbowpress.com
1 (866) 928-1240

Cover photo by Angela Lindstrom Photography.

ISBN: 978-1-4908-6751-9 (sc)
ISBN: 978-1-4908-6752-6 (hc)
ISBN: 978-1-4908-6750-2 (e)

Library of Congress Control Number: 2015901090

Printed in the United States of America.

WestBow Press rev. date: 2/2/2015

CONTENTS

Blessed art Thou, Lord, our God and King of the universe
who sanctifies us with Thy commandments and commands
us to engross ourselves in the words of the Torah.
It is to Thee, God, that this book is dedicated.

ACKNOWLEDGMENTS

I would love to do more than merely acknowledge every person and place that has helped me through this journey of searching the Hebraic roots of Christianity. However, there could not be enough trees in the forests to make enough paper for me to pen my gratitude to its fullest measure, so suffice it to say these paragraphs are an understatement of my sincere gratitude.

I would like to thank my pastor, Gregg Donnelley, Pastor Dominic Broda of Maple Plain Community Church, and Pastor Bruce Olson, along with Dr. Dean Ericson of Crown College in Minnesota, who were essential in helping me kick-start the writing process when I found myself without words. I would also like to thank Scott Alexander for giving me priceless advice that I wholly relied upon throughout my graduate studies.

I have been blessed by the opportunities to study the Jewish culture and my Hebraic roots in the Holy Land of Israel thanks to Day Spring Bible College in Chicago, Illinois. One of the greatest blessings I have received since I embarked upon this study is the friendships I have made within the Jewish community. From the first Orthodox woman I met on the way to Israel, Esther, who has inspired me more than she will ever know, to the Monday night group of messianic Jews and Torah-observant Christians with whom I have studied for the last two years, I am greatly indebted. I extend my deepest thanks to Pastor Jay Christianson of Issachar Community for taking me on as *talmida*.

Numerous friends and family have made this study an epic journey, primarily my husband, who has been so patient, encouraging, and understanding during all my studies. His words have kept me focused on why I study; that is, to show myself approved, rightly handling the Word of Truth.

It is for my children that I persevered in hopes of inspiring them to embark on such an undertaking. I am grateful for all their anointed words, particularly those of my son, Pastor Joe, and his insisting that I "be strong and courageous" and "focused" and that I "double up" as much as possible; these words have forever changed my life. Had Marcia not inspired me and Joanna not reminded me repeatedly of the learning ability of her first-grade students, I am not certain I would have made the first effort toward this writing. They have truly inspired me to learn, follow, and speak up. The love of Christ that I have received from my home church, Maple Plain Community Church, has carried me through this journey.

I am so grateful that my dad taught me to seek the truth and meaning in all things and for my friends and fellow Bible scholars with whom I have studied—LuAnn, Cindy, Jeannie, and Boni—who continued to challenge me to seek that truth. My mom, my cheerleader, and my friend never doubted my journey would take me here and has truly inspired me to find the freedom within the text. LuAnn is a true friend, fellow sojourner, and perfect mentor who has kept me accountable for my progress, encouraged me, and tested me from the very beginning of this journey to the very end, in the United States and in the Holy Land of Israel.

I pray all will be as blessed by this exploration of the Hebraic roots of Christianity as I have been.

DEFINITIONS OF TERMS

Aggadah – Nonlegal rabbinic teaching

Aliyah – Refers to one of seven parts of the parsha

Aliyot – Plural of aliyah

Ammora – Singular of amora'im

Amora'im – Those who contributed to the writing of the Gemara

Brit Chadasha – Refers to the New Testament

Haftarah – Refers to the part of any parsha that is read from the books of the prophets

Mezuzah – A small, decorative box for holding Shema, which is posted on the doorposts and the gates of homes and hotels

Midrash – A collection of commentaries on the Torah and its concepts. Midrash Rabbah means "The Great Midrash"

Midrashim – Plural of Midrash

Mikvah – Ritual bath for spiritual and ritual cleansing

Mitzvah – A commandment

Mitzvot – Plural of mitzvah

Parashot – Plural of parsha

Parsha – Meaning portion; also called Parashah

Sedarim – Section of the Mishnah

Shema – Scripture read daily, including Deuteronomy 6:4–9, 11:13–21, and Numbers 15:37–41

Talmud – The combined Mishnah and Gemara

Tanna – Singular of tannaim

Tannaim – Teachers quoted in the Mishnah; not to be confused with the amora'im, who contributed to Mishnah

Tefillah – More than prayer or worship, an intimate sharing of heart and soul

Tefillin – Phylacteries or boxes containing Shema and worn on the head and the upper arm during morning and evening prayers

Torah – The Torah includes the first five books of the Old Testament: Genesis, Exodus, Leviticus, Numbers, and Deuteronomy

Tzitzit – The tassels that hang on the corners of their garments

OBJECTIVES

Objectives of this research include the following:

- to uncover the meaning of the Law to the Jewish people in Moses' day
- to understand the meaning of the law to the people of Israel today
- to search for the unity of the Old Testament and New Testament
- to see the images of Jesus Christ in the Torah
- to access the extent to which the law of Moses should affect the life of a Christian
- to experience the freedom in the Torah

CHAPTER 1

Introduction to the Problem

The Israelites were slaves and held captive by Pharaoh, so God sent a savior to bring them to the land of promise, a land He promised to their ancestors, a land of freedom. More than a thousand years later, humanity was once again lost and searching for freedom. This time the slavery was to sin. Just as the Israelites wandered in the wilderness on their way to the Promised Land, we also are wandering in a wilderness on our way to the eternal Promised Land: heaven. As the inevitable quest for freedom is unending, so is the freedom of the Torah as taught by Moses and reiterated by Jesus, the Messiah. Facing many of the same challenges as the Israelites, fighting the same fears, there is much we can learn when we search the Torah for freedom.

Jesus was Jewish, the gospel is Jewish, and the root of Christianity is Jewish, making it beneficial to understand the historical context in which the Torah was written. Contextual study of the Old Testament Scriptures is not needed to acquire salvation but to grasp the full blessing and applicability, as well as experience the freedom found in the truth of the text. This is where one's hermeneutic should begin.

Research shows the following:

- Unity was in the testimonies given by Moses, Paul, and Jesus.
- All preached that the same law that applied to the Jew, at times, applies to the Gentile, the native, and the stranger that sojourn together.
- All Scripture is inspired, relevant, and useful.

In considering the text and stories of the Old Testament, many questions come to mind. Why is there an Old Testament at all? Why would a compassionate, loving Creator allow His chosen people, the Israelites, to be prisoners of Egypt? Why did the people of Israel wander for forty years on an eleven-day journey? Do you ever feel like you are wandering in a wilderness alone? Are you in search of the same freedom the children of Israel sought? Are you looking for a life filled with promise? Moses expounded on freedom in the book of Deuteronomy. He explained exactly where to find freedom and how to get there. He clearly spoke to the Jew and the foreigner. The question is this: does He speak to the Christian as well? This book examines the roots of Christianity to discover how our Jewish history, as taught since the time of Moses, can and should affect the daily lives of Christians.

Freedom has been my quest in life since I came kicking and screaming from my mother's womb on Independence Day. It seems fitting, then, that I should write about the pursuit of true freedom. In fact, every birth is a fight for freedom, one that never ends. Most Americans spend their entire lives looking directly in the face of freedom and never recognize it. Others never look for it because they don't realize freedom is their choice. Like many kids, I grew up in the church, Sunday school, confirmation, and summer church camps, yet I didn't learn the true freedom I had in the gift of Christ. Although I was schooled in Old Testament stories, there was little, if any, attempt to make them applicable to my life. I thought the Scripture, particularly the Old Testament, while based on true stories, was little more than words on the pages of an extraordinary history book. The same is true for many other Christians today. Though I searched for it, it was always evasive. I was confused about the gospel and the truth of Christ in the church. It's no wonder, as I grew up in the day of hell and damnation coming from one pulpit and the drama of *Jesus Christ Superstar* from another. The pendulum swung far to the right and equally as far to the left. In an attempt to cover one lie, society tends to exaggerate or make up another. At times, the Scripture is silent, and at other times, it moves us out of our sometimes complacent comfort zones. It's not uncommon in Bible studies and Sunday school classes to see folks add to the meaning of Scriptures (eisegesis) so that the text eases their fears or fits better with a personal agenda. Eisegesis is easy for anyone to do when the text is just words on the pages of a bunch of disconnected books assembled so far back in history that nothing could be applicable today. It is now my desire to stimulate the passion God placed in everyone for His truth, to help others understand the unity of the Scriptures and to find freedom in the Law of Torah.

The Importance of the Study

Moses was a leader with a great battle to fight in the hearts of God's people. In Moses' day, the Egyptian beliefs were responsible for the bad theology and godlessness of the people. Today the new-age beliefs as espoused by TV show hosts and movie stars make it hard for some to accept the simplicity of the truth. It is hard for any of us to believe that less is more. Moses was asking his people to trade their many gods for one. That's not any different from what God is asking us to do today. We too can have gods for everything, just like the Israelites did. While the twenty-first-century gods are not typically solid-gold cows, they can be equally discouraging, deceptive, and destructive. In fact, most of the time, we don't realize what we've turned into gods. At times, we might worship a car, finances, or a job. Ministries can become more important than the Lord. Even our children, grandchildren, or a handicap can be gods in this day of greater image. We might think, *If my children go to the right school* ... or *If I sing in the church choir, I'll look like I have good character,* making that image a god worth striving toward. All these and more are the golden calves of the twenty-first century.

Perhaps you're at a point in your life when you want to be a good Christian but don't know what that entails. So once again, striving begins. This time, determine to find something emotional as you search for happiness and freedom. Yet it seems God's goal is not to make us happy; rather, He wants us to be holy. Happiness and freedom will follow as a by-product of holiness.

There is a popular Christian pop song teaching that the believer in Jesus is a friend of God, yet referring to God as a friend seems like another pendulum that is swinging too far in the wrong direction. In fact, a friend recently said that "being a friend of God" might be the greatest deception of all time. That is not to say that God does not call us friends, as the Scriptures surely tell us He has (John 15:14–15).

Nevertheless, when we dwell on only the grace of God, it's easy to forget what He asks of us in return. My friend John compared the concepts of being a friend of God to the concept of fearing God to receiving a memo to report to the boss's office. You know of this person though you never see him; he usually goes by the title CEO or president. You know he owns the business and could fire you or give you a raise. When he calls you into his office, you straighten your jacket, check your hair, and humbly approach. Your heart beats a little harder as you pray you haven't done something wrong. Maybe he noticed you completed that big project. Maybe he misunderstood something you said to a competitor. Maybe he knows how many hours you spent last week surfing the Internet while looking for that new car. Thoughts rush through your mind. Regret and anticipation fill your heart.

Now imagine that your boss is a friend with whom you play racquetball every Tuesday. Maybe he is your neighbor with whom you barbecue and socialize on the weekends. At work, he hangs out by your desk and talks about the kids' soccer games. When he calls you into his office now, what is your reaction? Do you still straighten your jacket or check your hair? Are you even concerned about how much time you spend on the Internet doing things you are not supposed to do? Complacency is easy to reach when reverence is absent. Today, do you get dressed up to go to church? Do you give thanks before or after your meals? Or do you assume that God knows you're thankful?

Yes, salvation comes by grace. Still, in response to the hell, fire, and brimstone sermons of years ago, we have apparently forgotten our Hebraic roots. We dwell on the concept of forgiveness no matter what and forget what we learned in our desert wanderings. Must Gentile Christians keep the Law of the Old Testament to be saved? Certainly not! The New Testament does not claim Gentile believers are required to be Torah observant. The New Testament repetitively affirms that it is "by grace you have been saved, through faith: and that not of yourselves, it is a gift of God" (Ephesians 2:8). Everyone who calls on the name of the Lord "will be saved" (Acts 2:21). When asked outright how to be saved, Paul and Silas said, "Believe in the Lord Jesus, and you will be saved" (Acts 16:31).

What is it, then, that God expects of us? The Jewish people believed the Torah was one of seven things created before heaven and earth.[1] The sages, also known as wise men, and rabbis of old differentiate 613 laws in the Torah.[2] It is overwhelming to think one might have to live up to such standards—so overwhelming, in fact, that many would think ignorance is bliss. Is it true that as long as one does not know the law, one is not accountable? Just because we don't know what the speed limit is in a certain area, does this mean we can't get a ticket when exceed it? If ignorance means we are not accountable, we might all want to close the books now and end the study in case we might be able to apply some plausible deniability.

I imagine some might fear they will find out they need to be circumcised in their old age or start farming to raise the required number of sacrifices. For those who are already anxious about this, let me reassure you that these are just a couple of those 613 laws that never have and never will be applicable to the Gentile. In fact, most of those 613 laws are applicable only to the Levite, or only in the land of Israel, or only while there is a temple and the sacrificial system is in place. That, however, doesn't preclude their relevance. After all, doesn't mere curiosity beg to know those that do apply?

According to the apostle John, a man will flee from God because his deeds are evil (John 3:19). People will super-spiritualize themselves and reject Christ because Satan spiritually blinds them. This is not because of the people or circumstances that influence our lives as much as it is due to our nature. Humanity is the largest hindrance to faith. That which keeps the Gentile from believing is the same thing that keeps the Jew from believing. It is because we are human, and our nature is sin.

This hindrance starts with how one views the origin of man. If one's worldview says that humans are products of evolution, there will be less need for a Savior—if there is a need at all. However, if one believes in a Creator, the concept of our responsibility to the Creator is a natural companion.[3] There are many Scriptures illuminating the corruption of

---

[1] Louis Ginzberg. *The Legends of the Jews*. Henrietta Szold, trans., Kindle ed. Philadelphia: Jewish Publication Society of America, 2010. Kindle locations 127–130.

[2] Rambam. Rabbi Berel Bell, translator. *Sefer HaMitzvos of the Rambam Volume 1*, Kindle ed. Brooklyn: Sichos In English, 2013.

[3] Charles C. Ryrie. *Survey of Bible Doctrine*. Chicago: Moody Publishers, 1989. Kindle location 100.

human nature. This corruption involves human intellect (2 Corinthians 4:4; Romans 1:28), conscience (1 Titus 4:2), will (Romans 1:28), heart (Ephesians 4:18), and total being (Romans 1:18–3:20). However, depravity does not mean we have no control of our actions or that indulging in sin is inevitable for all. It does mean sin extends to all people and all parts of all human beings, so there is nothing within the natural individual that can make him or her righteous in the eyes of God.[4]

It is time we stop blaming others and our surroundings for our spiritual complacency. The Scripture tells us we are to study, to show ourselves approved that we might correctly handle the Word of God (2 Timothy 2:15), which implies that we are responsible for making every effort to understand that which is expected of us. Do we need to be scholars to understand the grace of God? No. The gospel of salvation is simple enough for a child to understand and believe (Mark 10:15). Believing the gospel, however, is only the beginning. Jesus commissioned all believers to take the simplicity of the gospel to the ends of the earth (Matthew 28:19), but whether we communicate with a wink, a word, a picture, or oral speech, if the message becomes garbled, the point is lost.[5] If we do not study the Scripture, we will never understand the magnitude of God's grace, what it cost to make that grace available to all who choose to believe, or what God expects of us in return. Without understanding, clear communication will be lost.

In the simplest form, there are two very basic approaches to Christian theology concerning the relationship between the Old Testament and the New Testament. A liberal or more spiritualized approach to biblical interpretation might claim that none of the Old Testament applies except the laws explicitly restated in the New Testament. In other words, history does not apply. This is replacement theology or supersessionism. Proponents of this view generally maintain that the Christian church has replaced Israel and the Jews are no longer the Chosen People of God. Supersessionalism is a theological stance that downgrades Judaism and implies imperfection of the Old Testament.

---

[4] Ryrie. *Survey*, 1989, 111.

[5] William W. Klein and Craig Blomberg. *Introduction to Biblical Interpretation*. Nashville, Tennessee: Thomas Nelson, Inc., 2004, 475.

The opposing concept would come from one who interprets the Scriptures literally and uses a historical, grammatical hermeneutic. This interpretation would believe that all of the Old Testament applies in a historical-grammatical context. This hermeneutic is known as non-supersessionism. Advocates of non-supersessionism affirm that salvation is through faith in Jesus only and that a future mass conversion will result in the restoration of Israel prior to the millennium, based on Romans 11:26 and Isaiah 59:20, which states, "All of Israel will be saved." This group finds the value of the Torah in the life of Jesus and his disciples, citing convicting New Testament teaching from the Sermon on the Mount as evidence.

> Do not think that I came to abolish the Law or the Prophets; I did not come to abolish but to fulfill. For truly I say to you, until heaven and earth pass away, not the smallest letter or stroke shall pass from the Law until all is accomplished. Whoever then annuls one of the least of these commandments, and teaches others to do the same, shall be called least in the kingdom of heaven; but whoever keeps and teaches them, he shall be called great in the kingdom of heaven   —Matthew 5:17–19).

The first official document to reevaluate the relationship between Judaism and the church was the *Declaration on the Relationship of the Church to Non-Christian Religions*, written in 1965. This document, known as the *Nostra Aetate*, was issued at the Second Vatican Council.[6] Nostra Aetate was a foundational document that spurred other church bodies to issue statements and guidelines on Jewish-Christian relations.[7] This document emphasized a spiritual link between the Jews and Christians, specifically teaching the continuation of the covenant between God and

---

[6] Austin Flannery. *Declaration on the Relation of the Church to Non-Christian Relations, in Vatican II: The Conciliar and Post-Conciliar Documents, vol. 1.* Collegeville, Minnesota: Liturgical Press, 1984, 738–742.

[7] "Guidelines for Jewish-Christian Relations," issued by the 1988 General Convention. Regarding teachings from the Anglican Communion, see "Jews, Christians and Muslim: The Way of Dialogue," appendix 6 of the *Report of the Dogmatic and Pastoral Section* by the 1998 Lambeth Conference.

Israel, a non-supersessionalist view, citing Romans 9:4–5. The Nostra Aetate affirmed the Jewishness of Jesus and the apostles while disproving any Jewish guilt for the death of Jesus and repudiating all forms of persecution against Jews.

Christians, however, historically took the Pauline perspective on the law and emphasized the punitive and temporary nature of the law while marginalizing the notion of the law as life-giving or having a positive value after the coming of Christ.

Jesus' theology in the Sermon on the Mount teaches that the law of Moses is still applicable. Christians need not become fully Torah observant to express their reverence for Torah. One can still express a traditional Jewish love for the Scripture when speaking of how much Jesus loved the Torah. Just as Jesus and the disciples saw the Torah as a living tradition, so did the early rabbis. An early third-century commentary on Mishnah Avot teaches, "Whosoever studies Torah is free."[8]

Regarding the law in the Old Testament, Christians will embrace the Ten Commandments and understand that Jesus upheld the law. Traditional Judaism insists on the relevance of the law in maintaining a relationship with God. If churches want to articulate a theology that does not repeat traditional misconceptions, it will require a direct engagement with the Jewish tradition.

Historical Context

Several problems surround a proper interpretation of the Scripture. Considering the historical context is essential to a healthy hermeneutic. History begs the question "Where does learning start?" First, one needs to find the original meaning of the text, and then one needs to find that same meaning in the context of our own day. One does not have to be an expert to do the job of exegesis well. One only needs to be aware that any given text could not mean what it never would have meant to

---

[8] *Avot de-Rabbi Nathan.* This translation is from *The Fathers according to Rabbi Nathan.* Judah Goldin, trans. New Haven, Connecticut: Yale University Press, 1955, 2.

its author or his or her readers. While this basic rule does not always determine what the text really means, it oftentimes gives limits as to what it cannot mean.

Ryken describes a literary approach that "is a logical extension of what is commonly known as the grammatico-historical method of biblical interpretation. Both approaches insist that we must begin with the literal meaning of the words of the Bible as determined by the historical setting in which the authors wrote."[9] Ryken claims that this approach builds on what biblical scholars have done to recover the original intended meaning of the text. The Scripture cannot mean today what it never meant when it was written, and if this principle were abandoned, "there would be no normative, compelling criterion for discriminating between valid and invalid interpretations."[10] According to Wright, there is always bias when exegesis is done;[11] therefore, without context, Scripture can become anything but truth. Too often, tradition disregards history, observation, and archeological evidence.

Culture

Understanding the culture of the writer and the original reader is another challenge to address when interpreting Scripture. Some idioms can change the meaning of a story entirely. What is an idiom? *The World English Dictionary* defines an idiom as

> 1. A group of words whose meaning cannot be predicted from the meanings of the constituent words, as for example (it was raining cats and dogs). 2. Linguistic usage that is grammatical and natural to native speakers of a language. 3. The characteristic vocabulary or usage of

---

[9] Leland Ryken. *How to Read the Bible as Literature.* 7th ed. Grand Rapids: Zondervan, 1984, 9.

[10] Henry A. Virkler and Karelynne Gerber Ayayo. *Hermeneutics: Principles and Processes of Biblical Interpretation.* Grand Rapids: Baker, 1981, 80.

[11] N. T. Wright. *Paul: In Fresh Perspective.* Minneapolis: Fortress Press, 2009, 15.

a specific human group or subject. 4. The characteristic artistic style of an individual, school, or period.[12]

Take, for example, the phrase *pulling my leg* or *drop me a line.* These phrases may be used in a context that was never meant to be taken literally. Another idiom that argues well the study of history and cultural context is the word *tripping.* In the 1950s, if someone said he was "tripping," he would most likely be referring to a "slip, mistake, error, or blunder." In the 1970s, someone using the same word might have been referring to "an instance or period of being under the influence of a hallucinogenic drug." Today, a young adult might say that he or she is "tripping" over the loss of a friend, meaning that they were in an emotional state of "intense preoccupation."[13] Depending upon the context and the culture at the time, this one word can mean falling down, using drugs, or a particular obsessive behavior. Do we need to look for the author's intended meaning? The answer is, undoubtedly, yes. While a study of the origins of Christianity will not solve all the disputes over interpretations of specific texts, examination of the culture surrounding the events of history will lend wisdom.[14]

The events of the Old Testament had three specific effects. First, whatever significance any particular event had in the history of Israel's experience with God and the articulation of their faith (i.e., the Old Testament) cannot just evaporate at the beginning of the New Testament. In other words, what it meant then, it still means today. Second, in certain Old Testament events, additional meaning can be seen in light of a messianic Jesus, and third, additional meaning can be seen in New Testament events based on an understanding of the Old Testament culture.[15]

Rabbi Hirsch claims the Torah to be anthropological, not theological,

---

[12] Dictionary.com, LLC, sv "Idioms." http://dictionary.reference.com/browse/idiom?s=t (accessed May 5, 2014).

[13] Dictionary.com, LLC, sv "Tripping." http://dictionary.reference.com/browse/tripping (accessed June 7, 2010).

[14] Mark A. Noll. *Turning Points: Decisive Moments in the History of Christianity.* Third ed. Grand Rapids: Baker Academic, 2012, 7.

[15] Christopher J. H. Wright. *Knowing Jesus through the Old Testament.* Downers Grove: InterVarsity Press, 1992, 28.

as he considers the written and the oral Torah (the Talmud) inseparable.[16] For the Jews, the Torah is considered to be the rule of faith and has been for the last three thousand years, as they have been careful to do everything according to the law (Deuteronomy 31:10–12). God told Joshua to meditate on the law day and night and to be careful to do according to all that was written in it (Joshua 1:8). The New Testament writers believed the Torah was testimony to Jesus Christ, the perfect sacrifice that fulfilled the law,[17] as Paul reminded the early church that all Scripture is profitable for teaching, for reproof, for correction, and for training (2 Timothy 3:16). Thus, we can look to Ezra as an example. He came up from Babylon, his place of captivity. He was a teacher well versed in the law of Moses, given by God Himself. His lifestyle was an example to all. The Scripture explains that because Ezra had set his heart to study Torah, to live a life pleasing to God, and to teach what he learned to all who would listen that the king granted him everything he asked for (Ezra 7:6–10). No doubt, Ezra had God's favor.

Dan Juster writes,

> The reason we belabor a summary of the structure of Deuteronomy is to provide context for truly understanding the Torah. Since Torah is central to Judaism, a messianic Jew must gain an accurate understanding of Torah in general if he is to know how to relate his Jewish heritage to Christian theology.[18]

If that is true, and the Christian is truly "grafted in" (Romans 1:23) by God's grace, then this statement would be equally true for any Christian. Grunlan and Mayers insist that the study of history begins with the study of the people, and any study of people, should begin with their origin; "If

---

[16] Joseph Elias. *The World of Rabbi Hirsch: The Nineteen Letters. 2nd ed.* Jerusalem: Feldheim Publishers, 1996, 19.

[17] Gleason L. Archer. *A Survey of Old Testament: Introduction.* Chicago: Moody Press, 1994, 19.

[18] Dan Juster. *Jewish Roots: A Foundation of Biblical Theology.* Shippensburg: Destiny Image Messianic, 1995, 14.

theology is the queen of sciences, then anthropology is the crown princess. Because man is the apex of God's creation, it is in the study of man that we can learn of God."[19]

It seems that for Jesus and Paul, Deuteronomy was their favorite book of Torah. Daniel Block points out that Jesus and Paul agree; if one looks to the law as a way to salvation, it will lead to death, but if one looks at Torah as a guide to life, it will yield blessing.[20] Jesus and the disciples from the first century were Torah observant. They were raised in a culture that was adherent to the law. Since the Christian is being conformed to the image of Jesus (Romans 8:29), it is important to understand how Jesus was obedient to the Father's commands.[21]

Most have heard a cliché that goes something like "Wisdom cannot make us all leaders, but it will help us discern who not to follow." Had Joshua and Caleb blindly followed their friends, they would not have made it into the Promised Land either. I imagine Joshua was afraid and inclined to run in the other direction when he heard God calling him to action. God must have known his fear, as He saw fit to command him to be strong and courageous (Joshua 1:6). This was not a request. Before the end of the first chapter in the book of Joshua, God reiterates this three more times, in verses 7, 9, and 18.

This year, God reminds me of that commandment daily as I persevere to finish this written exploration of Torah. I had many excuses for why I should not or could not start. For years, I could not take the time away from raising my children. Then I could not afford it. I have even used the excuse that I am too old or too sick to study. It is always something different, but if we look for an excuse, we will always find one that seems right in our own eyes. Truth, however, tells us that these excuses are disobedience, and disobedience is sin to which we can be slaves (Romans 6:6); therefore, obedience brings freedom. Swindol and Zuck agree that

---

[19] Stephen A. Grunlan, Marvin K. Mayers. *Cultural Anthropology: A Christian Perspective.* Grand Rapids: Zondervan, 1979, 268.
[20] Daniel I Block. *How I Love Your Torah, O LORD! Studies in the Book of Deuteronomy.* Eugene, Oregon: Cascade Books, 2011, 20.
[21] William Mark Huey and J. K. McGee. *Hebraic Roots: An Introductory Study.* Downers Grove: InterVarsity Press, 1992, 1.

no one was more submissive or free than Jesus, and true freedom comes only through submission to the authority of God.[22]

What I found at the root of my captivity was fear. It was not that I was too tired, too old, or too sick. I was just plain afraid. I was afraid to engage, afraid to commit, and afraid to finish. When I was gently reminded that I "did not need legs to walk with the Lord," I realized being "gripped with fear" is not a new concept and has never been a viable excuse for intentional disobedience. Joshua trusted God and stepped out in faith in his battle and we can do the same.

History of Torah Study

The Jewish population reveres Ezra the Scribe as the second Moses based exclusively on the importance of his work to preserve the Jewish culture. Ezra organized the books of the Bible into a theological order.[23] The tradition of reading the Torah aloud dates back to Moses (Deuteronomy 31); however, the Talmud claims Ezra established the practice of reading the Torah more frequently than just during Sukkot (aka the Feast of Tabernacles).

There are two traditions about the public reading of the Torah. One tradition has the Torah divided into 155 portions called *parshot* (also known as *sidra*), which are read one portion per week over a three-year cycle. The Reform Jews and some Conservative Jews in Israel follow this cycle even today. The other tradition comes from Babylon. Here, they use fifty-four parshot, and they read the Torah in one year. In nonleap years, they would read a double portion during five weeks. Since the second century BC, the public reading of these portions has been continuous.

Each parsha has seven sections or *aliyot* (ascent). In the Orthodox synagogue, when the parsha is read aloud, the first section is always read by the priest, and descendant of Aaron, and the second section is read by a Levite, although the Reform congregations have eliminated the distinction between tribes.

---

[22] Charles R. Swindol, Roy B. Zuck. *Understanding Christian Theology*. Nashville: Thomas Nelson Publishers, 2003, 122.

[23] Tov Rose. *The Paranormal Seams of the Hebrew Bible,* Kindle ed. Amazon Digital Services, 2012. Kindle locations 32–35.

The custom of reading from the books of the prophets and the writings called the *Haftarah* (appendix B, "Tanak") dates back to the second century BC, during the time of Antiochus, who banned reading from the Torah but not reading from the prophets. The Haftarah portions were selected thematically to be complementary to the weekly Torah portion. When boys and girls celebrate their bar mitzvahs/bat mitzvahs, respectively, it is customary that they read from the Haftarah.

Historically, the Jews have excelled in Torah study and memorization. Teaching the children begins when they are very young. As they celebrate Passover, the very small children ask traditional questions like "Why do we celebrate Passover?" and "What is the meaning of the covenant?" The answers are given in story form, beginning with Egyptian slavery. Rabbis are not to accept a student before six years old, but after children turn six years old, the Talmud teaches, "Accept them, and stuff them with Torah like an ox."[24] *Bet sefer* is a time in a child's life between the ages of six and ten when he or she studies the Torah. As a general rule, these children have the entire Torah memorized by the time they turn ten years old. Some go on, then, to memorize the entire Old Testament by the time they are thirteen (a time known as *bet talmu*), and from there, they become rabbis themselves. The children beg to read Torah on Shabbat. It is epic to see the respect and love the Jews have for the Word of God as the Torah is removed from the ark and carried around the synagogue every week. The congregation rises to its feet, reaching out to touch or kiss the Word of God as it passes by. Abraham Cohen teaches that no one should withhold himself from the study of the Torah, even at the hour of death.[25] Talmud teaches that the study of the Torah is greater than the rebuilding of the temple.[26] The book of Deuteronomy is read during the Jewish months of Av, Elul, and Tishri. (See appendix A for Torah portions.)

As the Jews study the Torah, they interpret it using four methods.

---

[24] Israel W. Slotki and Simon Maurice. *Soncino Babylonian Talmud Baba Bathra*, Kindle ed. Teaneck, New Jersey: Talmudic Books, 2012. Kindle location 4077.

[25] Abraham Cohen, *Everyman's Talmud: The Major Teachings of the Rabbinic Sages.* New York: Schocken Books, Inc. Reprint edition, 1996, 136.

[26] Maurice Simon and Segal Moses Hirsch. *Soncino Babylonian Talmud Megillah and Shekalim,* Kindle ed. Teaneck, New Jersey: Talmudic Books, 2012, 16b. Kindle location 2917.

P'shat (meaning "simple"), refers to the plain meaning of the text or a grammatical-historical exegesis. *Remez* (meaning "hint") refers to a deeper truth. *Drash* or *midrash* (meaning "search") is used to search the text for a relationship to other biblical or nonbiblical text as well as an allegorical or homiletical application of the text. Drash requires eisegesis, reading one's own thoughts into a text, as well as exegesis. *Sod* (meaning "secret") uses numerical values to determine hidden meaning in text. Christians do not normally use these same methods to interpret the Scriptures, and while I certainly would not encourage someone to incorporate numerology into his or her hermeneutic, I do think it is helpful to understand how the Old Testament text was being used and interpreted in the culture in which Jesus was raised. These methods of interpretation had great influence on the sages, and the sages, in turn, had great influence on the people, the writers, and the theological beliefs of those living in the time of Jesus.

Organization of the Study

Christianity confirms that the Scripture, in its entirety, is the inspired Word of God and without error; therefore, the primary source for this study has been the divinely inspired Word of God. The secondary sources used have been the scholarly writings of the sages, to include the Talmud and the Mishnah. As a means to decipher the meaning of the text as written, other writings by historical theologians and contemporary messianic leaders are used. Other books and articles that are highly valued by those Jews who study Torah, Mishnah, and Talmud today are used as well.

The following chapters will interact with these authors and bring together the law of the Old Testament, the historical context in which it was originally written, and the grace and salvation of the New Testament to show the applicability of Torah to the life of the New Testament believer. Unity and freedom in the Hebraic roots of Christianity have been found.

My research began with the discovery of the literature currently used by the rabbis today. I discovered the annual Torah cycle as designed by Ezra some five hundred years before Jesus, and I began my study there. With each parsha or section of Torah, I searched extra-biblical texts as well as New Testament Scripture for reiteration and recapitulation of the text within that parasha. I then turned to the rabbinic sources for the historical context. I found concepts that were well-known to the Jews of Deuteronomy, Jesus, and the Jews today. These concepts involved appropriate behavior, Jewish holidays, and attitudes that would be in one's best interest to respect. The 613 mitzvot (commandments or laws) found in the Torah as compiled by Rambam have also been considered. I then looked to anthropological literature that helped define culturally based issues as opposed to those that are cross-cultural, cross-gender, or cross-generational. As I uncovered the various concepts of each parsha, one primary theme kept resurfacing: the concept of freedom. After searching the rabbinic literature, I went to contemporary Christian theologians for insights based on a Christian worldview. Knowing that Christians can have very differing opinions on the Torah, the place of national Israel, and the church in redemptive history, I looked to biblical scholars from a variety of theological backgrounds in hopes of gaining true understanding of the key concepts of the Torah portions as studied by the Jewish community to facilitate New Testament exegesis. Any attempt to expound on the entire Torah would be a life's work, one I hope to be working on until my death. However, for the purposes of this book, my research is limited to the book of Deuteronomy and the key concepts found in the law that can help shape the life and future of the world.

The remainder of this book then is written following the divisions that were made by Ezra the prophet and used in synagogues today around the world. Each section has been first examined for the plain meaning (Scripture itself). I then turned to the rabbinic theologians (secondary sources) to culminate the historical context and understanding. In places, I examined the use of the Hebrew language; other times, I considered the Jewish superstition, as this also aids in our understanding of the writer's intended meaning. In each parsha, I looked for the shadows of our Messiah (Jesus Christ). I searched for freedom in each parsha and its applicability to the Gentile, sojourner, and Christian. Each parasha concludes with a list of the commandments or laws mentioned within each parasha and the number given them by Rambam. These are further grouped by applicability according to First Fruits of Zion, a messianic Jewish ministry specializing in the study of Scripture from its historical, linguistic, and cultural context. In other words, these groups are how a typical messianic Jew might interpret the Scriptures' applicability. The orthodox Jew would uphold these laws to be saved, whereas the messianic Jew would uphold these laws to please God as they believe Jesus Christ's death on the cross atoned for all sin, setting the Christian free from the obligation of the law.

This research investigates more than what the people did, where was it done, and when was it done. It looks deeper into who did it, why or how they did it, and what that has to do with everyone else as it seeks the meaning of events and it aims to develop concepts that will be enlightening, in turn helping others make sense of historical experiences and find applicability to existing circumstances.

Jewish Calendar

The Jewish calendar is a lunar calendar, and every month begins on the new moon. The first day of every month is known as *Rosh Chodesh*. The lunar calendar loses eleven days every year to the solar calendar. To balance the lunar and solar years, Hillel established a fixed calendar in the fourth century. It is based on a very complex mathematical formula. The number of days in a month or number of months in the year is determined by the precise time of day that the moon is full. Hillel created a nineteen-year cycle to determine which years would have thirteen months.[27] The extra month is included in the third, sixth, eighth, eleventh, fourteenth, seventeenth, and nineteenth years. In the year 2017 (5777 in the Jewish calendar), the cycle will start again. According to the Jewish calendar, the number 5777 represents the years since creation. See the chart below for a comparison of the Jewish and Gregorian calendars.

Jewish Month	Gregorian Month
Nissan	March–April
Lyar	April–May
Sivan	May–June
Tammuz	June–July
Av	July–August
Elul	August–September

---

[27] Tracey R Rich. *Judaism 101: Jewish Calendar*. http://www.jewfaq.org/calendar. htm (accessed May 30, 2014).

Tishri	September–October
Heshvan	October–November
Kislev	November–December
Tevet	December–January
Shevat	January–February
Adar	February–March
Adar II	March–April

CHAPTER 2

Introduction to the Book of Deuteronomy

The book of Deuteronomy begins, "Across the Jordan in the land of Moab, Moses undertook to expound this Torah" (Deuteronomy 1:5). Many scholars believe that Moses expounded Torah in all seventy languages of humankind.[28] The sages take this from the seventy family groups named in Genesis 10 that were scattered at Babel in Genesis 11. Was Moses bilingual in seventy languages? Or did he speak in one language that was miraculously understood in seventy, as the disciples did at Pentecost when they began the new sect of Judaism known today as Christianity (Acts 2)? The Scripture doesn't make that clear, but what the text does say is that he spoke to everyone, implying that everyone would understand.

The sages refer to Deuteronomy as Mishnah Torah, which commonly translates as "repetition of the Torah." The English (Deuteronomy) comes from the Greek word *deutero nomos*, meaning "second law" based on the Hebrew word *devarim*.

From an evangelical perspective, one of the better studies of the treaty formed in Deuteronomy is Meredith Kline's book *Treaty of the Great King*. Kline argues that the structure of Deuteronomy follows exactly the structure of the international treaties in use in the early second millennium BC.[29] The book of Deuteronomy follows the general pattern of an

---

[28] Ginzberg. *Legends.* 2010, 772.

[29] Meredith Kline. *Treaty of the Great King: The Covenant Structure of Deuteronomy: Studies and Commentary.* Eerdmans: Wipf & Stock Pub, 1963, 7.

ancient Near Eastern covenant treaty document between a king and his servants.[30] In the book of Deuteronomy, we find the typical preamble in 1:1–5, a historical prologue in 1:6–3:26, the conventional obligations from 4:1–26:19, blessings and curses from 27:1–30:20, and a conclusion from 31:1–34:12. This structure implies that God would be the king and the Israelites would be his vassals.

The entire Torah has not been repeated; in fact, of the two hundred laws identified in Deuteronomy, seventy are new laws. The book of Deuteronomy begins on the plains of Moab by the Jordan across from Jericho (Numbers 36:13). Deuteronomy contains three speeches of Moses intended to convict the Israelites to be faithful. Moses speaks of God's past miracles, summarizes the covenant, and prepares the younger generation for the future in the Promised Land. The book is primarily composed of Moses' farewell speeches to the Israelites. It is believed that he started writing the book on the first of Shevat in the year 2488 (1273 BC) and concluded thirty-seven days later on the seventh of Adar, the day of Moses' passing. Moses knew they needed to be strong and courageous, as they would no longer see God's presence and daily miracles once they entered the Promised Land. The manna would stop, and they would need to plow, plant, and harvest. They would need to establish government and social relationships to help the poor and needy as well as maintain strong faith to avoid making the same mistakes their fathers had made in the past. Stressing the law and moral values would create the discipline needed to avoid the temptation of the pagans with whom they would soon have to live. This is Moses' final effort to make a difference in the people's future. It is the grand finale to point them in the direction of freedom. Throughout the book of Deuteronomy, the recurring themes that should permeate every believer's daily life are fear not and remember.

---

[30] Ibid., 110.

Words

"Devarim"
Deuteronomy 1:1–3:22

The first parsha of Devarim (Deuteronomy) begins five weeks before Moses died[31] by proclaiming, "These are the words (devarim) that Moses spoke before the children of Israel …" Recounting the last forty years of wandering in the wilderness, Moses reviews some of the laws of the Torah and adds about seventy more to the list. He rebukes the Jewish people so that they might learn from their past mistakes. Moses reminisces about what took place at Horeb, the appointment of the tribal leaders, Israel's refusal to enter the land because of the negative report of ten of the spies, the prohibition to attack Edom and Moab, the defeat of the kings Sichon and Og, and the division of the land for Reuben, Gad, and half the tribe of Manasseh.

Deuteronomy 1:5 informs us of the Israelites' location at the time of this parsha. "Across the Jordan in the land of Moab, Moses undertook to expound this law." The ancient midrash called Tanchuma interprets this to mean that Moses spoke the words of Deuteronomy in all seventy languages of mankind.[32] It is interesting to note that only forty years earlier, Moses begged God to send someone else to speak to Pharaoh. By Moses' own words, he claimed he was not a man of words. He feared the entire concept of public speaking. Now at the end of his life, he speaks about 20 percent of the Torah, not only in his own words but also in all the languages of humanity. Although he fears the people, he fears God more, and he is obedient in answering His call. Like Moses, we too have a choice to run when the task seems too much for us or to follow where God leads and fulfill our potential. This clarifies that we should always attempt to communicate God's truth to people clearly in an understandable manner. Sometimes, that means we need to break down the text and simplify concepts. Other times, we need to expound on the implications of differing understandings.

---

[31] Scherman, Rabbi Nosson; Rabbi Meir Zlotowitz. *The Chumash: Artscroll Series.* Stone edition on Deuteronomy 1. New York: Mesorah Publications, 2000, 938.
[32] Davis. *Metsudah Midrash,* 2004, 7.

Rashi adds, "Torah should be new in your eyes every day … Turn it over; turn it over again, for everything is in it" (Avoth 5.22.154).[33] It also shows us it is obligatory for all to teach the gospel to the entire world and at all opportunities. Does that mean we all should be missionaries in Yemen, India, or another third-world country? No, but I do think it we can all be a bit more bold to reach the lost within our sphere of influence.

In this parsha, we read about two negative commandments. In 1:12, Moses asks, "How can I alone bear the load and burden of you and your strife?" Aware that he will not be with these people in the Promised Land, he obviously feels it necessary to remind them to maintain a court system that follows the way of God, so he reminisces about when he called together the heads of the tribes. He says, "Choose wise and discerning and experienced men from your tribes, and I will appoint them as your heads" (v. 1:13). Moses goes on, telling the people, "You shall not show partiality in judgment; you shall hear the small and the great alike. You shall not fear man, for judgment is Gods. The case that is too hard for you, you shall bring to me, and I will hear it" (v. 17). Here, Moses reiterates Deuteronomy 3:21–22. "Do not fear them, for the Lord your God is the one fighting for you." This is the text where we find the two commands: not to appoint a judge who does not know the Torah and not to fear wicked people.

How can these laws be relevant to Christians? The former command applies to anyone responsible for appointing judges to a Torah court of law or to congregational leadership. In the United States of America, we do have the privilege to vote, and with that comes the responsibility to vote intelligently. That means if we choose to vote for a judge, we should do our homework on those judges that are running and choose one who is God-fearing. If we choose not to do the research, then we can choose to leave that page blank.

The latter applies to judges on a court of law and refers to fearing God more than fearing what the criminal on trial might do to him should he rule against the criminal.

---

[33] J. Israelstam, M. H. Segal, and H.M. Lazarus. *Soncino Babylonian Talmud Makkoth, Eduyyoth and Aboth,* Kindle ed. Teaneck, New Jersey: Talmudic Books, 2012. Kindle locations 7895–7896.

Moses' Rebuke (v. 1:1–8)

The midrash sees the book of Deuteronomy as a rebuke, citing several cases of deathbed rebuke.[34] The parsha begins in Deuteronomy 1:1. "These are the words which Moses spoke to all Israel across the Jordan in the wilderness, in the Arabah opposite Suph, between Paran and Tophel and Laban and Hazeroth and Dizahab." Why does Moses bring up places where they have traveled? Surely, they have been in other places as well. Then why does he limit this list to just these specific places? The sages of the Mishnah explain that each of the locations mentioned here is to remind the Israelites of events that took place in the desert. There is much symbolism to be found in the events, places (such as the Tabernacle[35]), and words used to teach God's truth. Moses wanted their immediate attention and he used experiences from their past to get it. In 1990, mentioning the day September 11 would have meant nothing to most people in the United States. Today, however, the mere mention of the numbers *911* brings to mind evil, chaos, tragedy, and survival.

Across the Jordan in the wilderness

"In the wilderness" would remind them of Exodus 17:3 when they complained, "Why, now, have you brought us up from Egypt, to kill us and our children and our livestock with thirst?" Moses called the place Massah U'Meribah because of the contention of the children of Israel and because of their test of God, saying, "Is God among us or not?" (v. 17:7). Massah U'Meribah literally means "test and contention." By naming the place after their bad behavior, Moses continually reminds them that God is living among them and that the proper way to express concern is through prayer and not through disrespectful challenges.

---

[34] Reuven Hammer. The Classic Midrash: Tannaitic Commentaries on the Bible Classics of Western Spirituality 1st ed. Mahwah, New Jersey: Paulist Press, 1995, 289.
[35] James Strong. *The Tabernacle of Israel: Its Structure and Symbolism*. Grand Rapids: Kregel Publications, 1987, 114.

In the Arabah

Rashi notes this is the name of a particular plain (Rashi to Genesis 14:6).[36] "In the Arabah," or "plain," as it says in some translations, is where the sin with the Moabite women and Ba'al Peor took place (Numbers 25). Balaam knew that sexual morality is a foundational belief of the Jewish people and that God would not tolerate this sin; therefore, Balaam told Balak the only way to curse Israel was to entice the men to bring the curse upon themselves. The Moabite women invited the men to eat and drink. After enough drink, the women seduced them into worshiping their Ba'al Peor idols.[37]

Opposite Suph: Suph, also known as the Sea of Reeds, is where the Israelites crossed over on dry ground (Exodus 14:11). "Were there no graves in Egypt?" Rabbi Hirsch explains that the purpose of Israel's wanderings was to prove that God is active and involved in the daily and sometimes trivial affairs of life as well as amazing events like the crossing of the Red Sea.[38]

Between Paran: This refers to the place where the sin of the spies in Numbers 13 took place. The most common sin of unbelief took place when the spies explicitly stated in verse 31, "We cannot ascend to that people for it is too strong for us!" The Chumash claims the bigger sin was spreading unbelief around the camp.

And Tophel and Laban: Rashi and Rabbi Yochanan agree there is no place in Scripture named Tophel and Laban. Rather, they would argue the words refer to the complaints about the manna (Numbers 10:12, 11:6), rendering Tophel calumny and Laban white.[39]

And Hazeroth: Korach's revolt against Moses took place near Hazeroth. Miriam was also afflicted with leprosy in Hazeroth for rebelling and slandering God's anointed. But the people of Israel did not learn from these events and still slandered the name of God.

Dizahav: Literally means "abundance of gold." It is true that God

---

[36] Scherman, Rashi. *Chumash*, 2000, 939.

[37] Scherman, Alshich. *Chumash*, 2000, 875.

[38] Scherman, Hirsch. *Chumash*, 2000, 381.

[39] Scherman, Rashi, Yochanan. *Chumash*, 2000, 939.

blessed Israel with an abundance of gold when they left Israel, and in turn, the Israelites used that gold, that gift from God, to make the golden calf.

The rabbinic literature agrees that this opening in Deuteronomy was given to the children of Israel to remind them of where they have been and from what they have been rescued. The incident of the golden calf did not bring an end to God's faithfulness. It only highlighted the need for their obedience and deliverance.[40] This should also be a reminder for the Christian, lest we forget where we have been and where we are going.

The Wickedness of Judah

The Haftarah portion for parsha Devarim is from Isaiah 1:1–27. This also illuminates the wickedness of Judah and the corruption that took place in the city. The wickedness was so great that the rabbis devoted an entire tractate of the Talmud to explaining the laws and consequences of such a rebellion.[41] This is a good reminder to all people that God requires more than burnt offerings, incense, and ritual law. According to verse 13, they are detestable to Him. Rather, God says in verse 16, "Wash and make yourselves clean. Take your evil deeds out of my sight; stop doing wrong. Learn to do right; seek justice. Defend the oppressed. Take up the cause of the fatherless; plead the case of the widow." Then, in an attempt to teach the people not to fear where God sends them, the Haftarah portion ends by reminding Israel that Zion will be delivered with justice. Hebrews 13:15 echoes the command to praise continually with a generous heart.

Fear Not

In this first portion of Devarim, the people ask, "Where can we go up? Our brethren have made our hearts melt, saying, 'The people are bigger and taller than we; the cities are large and fortified to heaven. And besides, we saw the sons of the Anakim there'" (Deuteronomy 1:28). Ten of the twelve

---

[40] Walter C. Kaiser, Jr. *Toward an Old Testament Theology*. Grand Rapids: Zondervan, 1979, 113.

[41] E. W. Kirzner. *Soncino Babylonian Talmud Baba Kamma,* Kindle ed. Teaneck, New Jersey: Talmudic Books, 2012. Kindle location 496.

spies lacked the faith needed to trust that God would give them this land. Their unbelief caused the people to cry out in fear.

Sidney Smith once said, "A great deal of talent is lost to the world for want of a little courage. Every day sends to their graves obscure men whose timidity prevented them from making the first effort."[42] There is discussion throughout the Scriptures on fear. Fear can drown even the most powerful of men. Solomon and Elijah were two great men who felt this despair when they feared the thing most central to their identity as human beings was lost.[43] This too is addressed in the Haftarah portion "for He (God) has said, I will never desert you, nor will I ever forsake you" (Hebrews 13:6). St. Augustine was clearly convinced that God was present everywhere. Recalling Jeremiah 23:24, he wrote, "For where outside heaven and earth can I go that from thence my God may come into me who has said, I fill heaven and earth?"[44] For the Israelites, and most people today, the first effort must be faith in the power of God to do what He said He would do.

Fear of Wicked People

Moses commanded the leaders of the tribes not to show partiality to others based on their position of influence or power. This implies that there may have been those judges or leaders who would base their judgment on fear of those with more power. The Talmud made a close connection between ethics and law, arguing that the Jews regarded civil and criminal law as Scripture. They saw it as divinely inspired.[45]

James, the brother of Jesus, saw partiality as sin (James 2:9). Jesus was well-known for His impartiality, as He would choose to dine with the sinners, tax collectors, or sages (Matthew 22:16). Moses told the leaders and all the people, "Do not fear them, for the Lord your God is the one fighting for you" (Deuteronomy 3:21–22). This is a command we hear

---

[42] Sydney Smith. *Brainy Quote.com* (accessed May 20, 2014). http://www.brainy-quote.com/quotes/quotes/s/sydneysmit100934.html.

[43] Boruch Clinton. *Midrash—Bringing Torah to Life*, Kindle ed. Marbitz: Media, 2012. Kindle location 494.

[44] St. Augustine and Wyatt North, trans. *The Life and Writings of Saint Augustine*, Kindle ed. Wyatt Noth Publishing, 2012. Kindle location 2209.

[45] Kirzner. *Baba Kamma*, 2012. Kindle location 275.

repeated over 130 times in the Scriptures with five of those occurrences in this parsha alone. Paul tells us in Romans 8:15, "For you have not received a spirit of slavery leading to fear again, but you have received a spirit of adoption as sons by which we cry out, Abba! Father!" So often, fear became an idol in the lives of the Jews. Even today, many find themselves crippled by fear: fear of the giants, fear of failure, or fear of rejection. Such fear can be so intense that it can confine one to the boundaries of their home. Fear certainly kept the Israelites from entering the Promised Land. After forty years of eating manna and watching the elders die in the wilderness, Moses addresses the new generation to encourage them to be strong and courageous. He carefully constructs his words to remind the Israelites of what God has done for them in hopes of freeing them from the bondage of fear.

The Ninth of Av

This portion of Devarim is read on the Sabbath that precedes the ninth of Av on the Jewish calendar. The ninth of Av is known as Tisha B'Av. Tisha B'Av is a fast day, the climax of a three-week mourning period. During this fast, eating and drinking are forbidden. The Jew does not bathe, use moisturizing creams or oils, wear leather shoes, or have marital relations.[46] The basic idea is to minimize pleasure so as to feel the distresses of the body, convicting oneself to a point of sincere sorrow over the historical events of this day.

The ninth of Av is known as a day during which no good can happen. Throughout Jewish history, many tragedies befell the Jewish people on this day. Primarily, Tisha B'Av mourns the loss of the temples in Jerusalem. Even greater is the loss of feeling God's presence. Tragedies that the Jewish people have suffered on the ninth of Av include[47]

- the incident of the spies returning in fear with a negative report of the Promised Land

---

[46] Karesh and Hurvitz. *Encyclopedia of Judaism,* 2006. Kindle location 3530.

[47] My Jewish Learning. "Tisha B'Av History" (accessed May 20, 2014). http://www.myjewishlearning.com/holidays/Jewish_Holidays/Tisha_BAv/Ideas_and_Beliefs.shtml.

- the destruction of the first temple in Jerusalem by the Babylonians in 586 BC
- the destruction of the second temple in Jerusalem by the Romans in AD 70
- the fall of Betar and the end of the Bar Kochba revolt against the Romans in AD 135
- the declared First Crusade by Pope Urban II, during which tens of thousands of Jews died and many Jewish communities were obliterated
- the expulsion of the Jews of England 1290
- the expulsion of the Jews of Spain 1492
- the onset of World War I in 1914 when Russia declared war on Germany; German resentment of the Treaty of Versailles set the stage for World War II and the Holocaust
- the beginning of deportation of Jews from the Warsaw Ghetto on Tisha B'Av

What are the giants that so many face today? What is it that causes such fear if God does not give a spirit of fear? He who resurrected Christ from the grave will rescue those who believe as well. God, who cared for the sparrow, cares for His children. What can anyone or anything do to one who is protected by God? Fear, then, is the opposite of faith. For a person of faith, fear is irrational.

Mitzvot[48]

Applies to anyone responsible for appointing judges to a Torah court of law.

- N284 – Deuteronomy 1:13 – Do not appoint a judge who is not knowledgeable of the Torah

Applies to judges on a Torah court of law.

- N276 – Deuteronomy 1:17 – Do not fear wicked people.

---

[48] Numbered by Rambam. Grouped by applicability according to First Fruits of Zion.

CHAPTER 3

And I Pleaded

"Va'etchanan"
Deuteronomy 3:23–7:11

Va'etchanan is the forty-fifth portion from the Torah and the second portion of Deuteronomy. Va'etchanan means "and I besought" or "and I pleaded." This name comes from the first verse of the parsha, which says, "I also pleaded with the Lord at that time" (Deuteronomy 3:23). Va'etchanan marks the end of the historical prologue of Deuteronomy.

In this portion of Deuteronomy, Moses views Canaan from Pisgah and prays to be allowed to enter the Promised Land (3:23). Moses instructs Israel to obey (4:1) and then establishes the cities of refuge east of the Jordan (4:41). Moses repeats the Ten Commandments (5:1) and then reminds the people of how he interceded for them (5:22). Moses then gives them the great commandment to love the Lord their God with all their heart and with all their soul and with all their mind (6:4–9). The parsha concludes as Moses warns the Israelites of what would happen if they disobeyed (6:10) and cautions them about the responsibility of being a chosen people. He predicts that future generations will worship other gods and be exiled from the land, but that they would again seek God from the Diaspora.

This portion also contains some of the most fundamental passages in the Torah, including the Ten Commandments, the Shema, the commandments of the tefillin and mezuzah, and the teaching of the Torah.

Moses' Prayer

Deuteronomy 4 makes it clear that when the Jewish people are obedient to the Torah, God will bless them, and prayer is an important part of obedience. In the parsha, Va'etchanan, Moses pleaded to enter the Promised Land. The word we translate as "pleaded" or "implored" is one of ten terms for *prayer*. This word is used when one seeks unmerited favor. The Chumash states that Moses meant this to inspire the Israelites to persevere in prayer, claiming that the "gates of tears" are always open.[49]

Moses knows God will pour out His blessings on those who are faithful and will repay those who are not. Here, Moses repeats the Ten Commandments given at Mount Sinai, ensuring that those entering this land understand that these commandments were not meant only for their fathers and grandfathers. With almost forty years having passed, Moses makes it clear that the Ten Commandments apply to all future generations.[50] This covenant included 613 commandments and was to be for the entire Jewish nation for all time. Deuteronomy 4:5 explains that these commandments are given for them to follow when they enter the Promised Land, as many could not be observed in the wilderness or Babylon.

The Ten Commandments

The general content of the Ten Commandments in Deuteronomy 5 is similar to Exodus 20 but not identical. Perhaps this is because Moses is retelling the story in Deuteronomy, whereas in Exodus it is the voice of God speaking. In Exodus, the people are to "remember" the Sabbath. In Deuteronomy, Moses tells the people to "observe" the Sabbath. Remembering what the Sabbath represents is important, as it commemorates creation and their freedom from the slavery they knew in Egypt. Observing the Sabbath, on the other hand, would suggest obedience is the goal and is applicable to all people of all times.

In the Chumash, chapter 5, verse 17, Moses uses the word "vain," whereas in Exodus the word "false" is used. Vain is a little more inclusive,

---

[49] Scherman. Midrash. *Chumash,* 2000, 959.
[50] Scherman. *Chumash,* 2000, 969.

indicating that lying is wrong under all circumstances.[51] There is also a difference in verse numbers between Exodus and Deuteronomy as well as from the Chumash and other English translations. Verses 17–20 in the English translation are combined into one verse in the Hebrew text as Moses connects the prohibitions that deal with human relationships with the word "and" to imply that all sin against people is equally wrong. Sins against another man's wife, marriage, property, or even honor are all considered equally grave.

Rabbi Hirsch argues that the climax of the Ten Commandments is the law against the criminal thought claiming that the longing for others' possessions is equally criminal. R' Hirsch explains, "The surest protection against crime is the abolition from one's mind of the criminal thought or any incitement to it."[52] In the New Testament, James explains that whoever is guilty of one crime is guilty of them all (2:10). This is why Paul stresses the need to take captive every thought to the obedience of Christ (2 Corinthians 10:5). He knows that every sin starts in the mind. According to the sages, even the fantasy of such a sin was considered sinful.[53] Paul reminds the reader in Romans 3:10 that there is not one that is righteous, not even one. Salvation, however, is a gift from God. It is not of works, lest any man should become prideful (Ephesians 2:8–9) and profitable for teaching and training in righteousness (2 Timothy 3:16).

The Shema

The Shema consists of three biblical passages (Deuteronomy 6:4–9; 11:13–21; Numbers 15:37–41). The first part of the Shema is found in parsha Va'etchanan. *Sh'ma Yis'ra'eil Adonai Eloheinu Adonai echad.* These words are part of a prayer known today as the Shema. Jews live with the Shema and die with the Shema. According to the testimonies of those who witnessed the gassings at Auschwitz, the words of the Shema were the last thing heard from the Jews before death. The Shema became a regular part

---

[51] Ibid.
[52] Ibid.
[53] Scherman, Rambam. *Chumash,* 2000, 971.

of the prayer service during the second temple period.[54] It articulates the obligation to study the Torah, obey the Torah, and teach the Torah.

Sh'ma or Shema means "hear," and this text is sometimes referred to as the central creed of Judaism, though it is not really a creed but Scripture. It is a command to recite the Shema twice daily and is applicable to Jewish men in every time and place. The Shema is the witness that is brought to the world by God. Included in the Shema is Deuteronomy 6:4–10.

> Hear, O Israel! The Lord is our God, the Lord is one! You shall love the Lord your God with all your heart and with all your soul and with all your might. These words, which I am commanding you today, shall be on your heart. You shall teach them diligently to your sons and shall talk of them when you sit in your house and when you walk by the way and when you lie down and when you rise up. You shall bind them as a sign on your hand and they shall be as frontals on your forehead. You shall write them on the doorposts of your house and on your gates. Then it shall come about when the Lord your God brings you into the land which He swore to your fathers, Abraham, Isaac and Jacob, to give you, great and splendid cities which you did not build.

The words "Hear, O Israel" are also translated as "Obey, Israel." Rambam (Maimonides) lists the commandments in logical order beginning with the most important. According to Sefer HaMitzvot, believing in God is most central to the Jewish belief, followed closely by the command to acknowledge the oneness of God and to love Him with all of oneself.[55]

Deuteronomy 6:4–5 reads, "Hear, O Israel: Yahweh our Elohim, Yahweh is one. Love Yahweh your *Elohim* with all your heart and with all your soul and with all your strength."[56] The term *Yahweh* functions more as the personal name of Israel's God and is used 6,800 times in the Old

---

[54] Steinsaltz. *The Essential Talmud,* 2006, 104.

[55] Rambam. *HaMitzvos Vol. 1,* 2013.

[56] Hays and Longman III. *The Message of the Prophets,* 2010. Kindle location 151.

Testament. Therefore, Rambam attests that when one meditates on God's creation and His wondrous deeds, one will come to love and worship Him with all of his or her heart.[57] Some sages interpret the heart as a metaphor for the seat of craving and inspiration, claiming that one needs to love God with both the evil and good inclinations[58] even to the point of death.[59]

The need for prayer and its effectiveness are never in doubt. As Moses built the temple in the wilderness as a home for the Spirit of God (Shekinah) and a place to pray, it is doubtful he knew then that one day the Messiah would build the body of the believer to be the temple (1 Corinthians 6:9). Yet it is easy to see the shadows of the New Testament in the construction of the temple of Moses.[60] God must have known that daily prayer would be a struggle. Jesus prayed in the garden and beseeched His disciples to pray. Paul reminds the believer to pray continually and without ceasing (1 Thessalonians 5:16–17). Prayer will not be vain, as God hears the prayer of the righteous and sees their tears (2 Kings 20:4–5).

Tefillin

Tefillin, also known as phylacteries, are little boxes containing Shema and strapped to the forehead and to the arms. Some argue that the ritual of strapping these Scriptures to the body were never meant to be taken literally; rather, they were meant to be interpreted metaphorically, keeping God's Word in our minds and in our hands. However, that does not disqualify a literal ritual. Yigael Yadin led the Institute of Archeology at The Hebrew University in Jerusalem in 1970. While excavating at Masada, this archeologist discovered well-preserved tefillin with the Torah portions dating back to the first century.[61] The tefillin are to be reminders of the covenant obligations. It is commanded that every man shall write the

---

[57] Scherman, Ramabam. *Chumash*, 2000, 973.

[58] Rabbi M. Silbermann. Pentateuch with Targum Onkelos and Rashi's Commentary: Torah, The Book of Devarim, Volume V. Hebrew / English. BN Publishing, 2011, 37.

[59] Maurice Simon. *Soncino Babylonian Talmud: Berakoth*, Kindle ed. Teaneck, New Jersey: Talmudic Books, 54a. Kindle location 11484.

[60] M. D. DeHaan. *The Tabernacle*. Grand Rapids: Zondervan Publishing, 1955, 104.

[61] Yigael Yadin. Masada: Herod's Fortress and the Zealot's Last Stand, 1st ed. Random House, 1966.

Shema, insert it into tefillin, and wear them on the upper arm and on the head, above the hairline, directly between the eyes (Exodus 13:16).

Mezuzah

Again, the mandate is to hand-write the text of the Shema, insert the Scripture into a small container called a mezuzah, and attach it to the doorposts of the house and on the gates. The Torah does not say which Scriptures are to be used, but tradition tells us that Deuteronomy 6:10 was used for the tefillin and the mezuzah. This is a physical indication that the home where one finds the mezuzah is a Torah-observant home. When one goes out, it should be a reminder that there is an obligation to conduct oneself as a child of God. There is no prohibition against the Gentile fixing a mezuzah; it should be kept in mind that it is a reminder of what God would expect of us. This text should also remind Christians to keep the Word of God at the forefront of their mind, ever-ready to give a defense for the hope found in Christ (1 Peter 3:15).

Teach Your Children

The Shema commands, "You shall teach them diligently to your sons and you shall you shall speak of them (the wondrous deeds of God) when you sit at home, and when you walk along the way, and when you lie down and when you rise up." In other words, teaching Torah is to be a full-time job for all: not just in the church, not just in the home, not only to the children, but also to anyone who will listen. *V'shinantam* translates to "teach diligently," though the literal meaning is "review it again and again" until becoming extremely well versed in Torah.[62] Rashi asked the question about verse 7, "Who are your sons?" The word *ben*, universally translated as "sons," can also mean "student," "child," "children," "stranger," "steward," and more. Therefore, Rashi concludes that you shall teach the mitzvot diligently to your students. Moses implied that the fear of God

---

[62] Hayim H. Donin. *To Pray as a Jew: A Guide to the Prayer Book and the Synagogue Service*, Kindle ed. Jerusalem: Basic Books, 2001, location 1725.

is an essential outcome of Torah study.[63] Meditation that does not lead to commitment and action is entirely inadequate. The requirement to teach is to fear God and keep His commandments. The work of the teacher is then to prepare God's people for works of service.[64] One might assume that Christian teaching is moral in and of itself. Yet faith in Christ and morality are two different issues. If we do not teach our young principles of moral decision making that reflect our faith (Torah), then whose principles will they learn?[65]

According to Madeline Hunter and Dr. Katheryn Webb, one of the key elements of effective Christian teaching is to remember that from a biblical standpoint that teaching and learning cannot be separated. We cannot teach if we stop learning, and we cannot stop learning when we teach.[66] The three primary duties of a teacher are to present the truth; to learn, practice, and teach the Word; and to equip the saints for service. The latter involves encouraging the student to do the same. Rambam argues that it is incumbent on every scholar to teach.[67] This is also seen in the New Testament and known as the Great Commission, as found in Matthew 28:19. "Go therefore and make disciples of all the nations, baptizing them in the name of the Father and the Son and the Holy Spirit, teaching them to observe all that I commanded you; and lo, I am with you always, even to the end of the age." The Chumash recognizes that the priority a person gives to the education of his children demonstrates his personal devotion to the Torah.[68] The rabbis agree that the Torah and service of God should be the main topic of every discussion and the objective of every task. Reciting the Shema morning and night will keep one focused on pleasing God. Bechor Shor (a French tosafist, exegete, and poet who flourished late in the

---

[63] Scherman. Or HaChaim. *Chumash*, 2000, 961.

[64] William R. Yount. *Created to Learn: A Christian Teacher's Introduction to Educational Psychology.* Nashville, Tennessee: Broadman & Holman Publishers, 1996, 253.

[65] Yount. *Created to Learn*, 1996, 103.

[66] According to Madeline Hunter and Dr. Katheryn Webb, Dynamic Teaching Class, September 11, 2008.

[67] Rambam: *Talmud Torah 1:2*, http://www.chabad.org/library/article_cdo/aid/910973/jewish/Talmud-Torah-Chapter-One.htm (accessed May 29, 2014).

[68] Scherman. *Chumash,* 2000, 975.

twelfth century) tells us "by occupying yourself with Torah study in every possible situation, you will reach your goal of loving God."[69]

The Haftarah portion for Va'etchanan (Isaiah 40:1–26) is one of the seven Sabbaths between Tisha B'Av and Rosh Hashanah, called "the seven of consolation." As with the three haftaros of affliction, the seven of consolation are Scriptures, read from the later chapters of Isaiah and are not related to the sidra. We do, however, see the theme of teaching and proclaiming the good news repeated here:

> A voice says, "Call out." Then he answered, "What shall I call out?" All flesh is grass, and all its loveliness is like the flower of the field. The grass withers, the flower fades, when the breath of the Lord blows upon it; surely the people are grass. The grass withers, the flower fades, but the word of our God stands forever. Get yourself up on a high mountain, O Zion, bearer of good news, Lift up your voice mightily, O Jerusalem, bearer of good news; Lift *it* up, do not fear. Say to the cities of Judah, "Here is your God!" —Isaiah 40:1–8

The Haftarah ends with the big picture of comfort for Jerusalem that only God can give.

The Great Commission is the climax of the responsibility to teach. "Go therefore, and make disciples of all the nations, baptizing them in the name of the Father and the Son and the Holy Spirit, teaching them to observe all that I commanded you" (Matthew 29:19–20). Therefore, what is the "good news" that every person is called to teach? Teach them it is "by grace you have been saved through faith in Jesus Christ" (Ephesians 2:8). Martin Luther seemed to grieve over those who did not teach the gospel, saying sermons ramble on, but there ought to be nothing else but the proclamation of Christ.[70]

---

[69] Scherman. Bechor Shor. *Chumash*, 2000, 975.
[70] Martin Luther. *Treatise on Good Works*, Kindle ed. Public Domain Books, 2009. Kindle location 695.

Faithfulness of God

Comfort ultimately comes through the one and only son of God, who was born and died so that all who believe will be saved, proving again that God is faithful.

In 1962 Arthur Combs wrote, "People are always motivated; in fact, they are never unmotivated, they may not be motivated to do what we would prefer they do, but it can never be truly said that they are unmotivated."[71] Scripture reveals to us fifty-seven different teaching methods used by Jesus and forty-two visual and audio aids.[72] Carl Rogers writes in his book *Freedom to Learn for the 80's*, "In my view education should evoke real learning ... not the lifeless, sterile, futile, quickly forgotten stuff which is crammed into the mind of the poor helpless individual tied to his seat by ironclad bonds of conformity!"[73] In Christian education, "knowing the right answer" is not good enough. Jesus calls us to a kingdom lifestyle.[74] Bruner says, "We teach a subject not to produce little living libraries on that subject, but rather to get students to think for himself ... to take part in the process of knowledge-getting. Knowing is a process, not a product."[75]

Teaching Torah is a job for every disciple of Jesus in the same way it is incumbent upon every believer to spread the gospel (Matthew 28:16–20), and when properly presented, the Torah should be an avenue to Jesus. It is a natural fit with the gospel of salvation. The Christian is called to emulate Jesus who dedicated his life to proclaiming the gospel and teaching the ways of Torah.

---

[71] Arthur Comes. "Motivation and the Growth of Self," in Perceiving, Behaving, and Becoming: The Association for Supervision and Curriculum Development Yearbook, Washington, DC: National Education Association, 1962, 83–98, quoted in Yount, *Created to Learn*, 286.

[72] Roy B. Zuck. *Teaching as Jesus Taught*. Eugene, Oregon: Wipf and Stock Publishers, 2002, 179–180.

[73] Carl Rogers. *Freedom to Learn for the 80's*. Columbus, Ohio: Merill, 1983, 121, quoted in William R. Yount, *Created to Learn*. Nashville, Tennessee: Broadman & Holman Publishers, 1996, 235.

[74] Yount. *Created to Learn*, 1996, 234.

[75] Robert E. Slavin. *Educational Psychology: Theory and Practice*. Boston: Allyn and Bacon, 1994, 225, quoted in Yount, *Created to Learn*, 201.

Mitzvot[76]

Applies to Jews and God-fearing Gentile believers, both men and women, in every time and place.

- N266 – Deuteronomy 5:21 – Not to desire that which belongs to one's neighbor
- P3 – Deuteronomy 6:5 – Loving God
- P11 – Deuteronomy 6:7 – Studying and teaching Torah
- P2 – Deuteronomy 6:4 – Unity of God to acknowledge the oneness of God

Applies to everyone in every time and place.

- N64 – Deuteronomy 6:16 – Not testing His promises and warnings or demanding signs from a known prophet
- N50 – Deuteronomy 7:2 – Not showing mercy or favor to idolaters

Applies to Jewish men in every time and place.

- P10 – Deuteronomy 6:7 – Reading the Shema twice daily, morning and night
- P13 – Deuteronomy 6:8 – Wearing tefillin on the hand
- P12 – Deuteronomy 6:8 – Wearing tefillin on the head
- P15 – Deuteronomy 6:9 – Affixing a mezuzah on one's doorpost
- N52 – Deuteronomy 7:3 – Not intermarrying with a heretic

Applies to Jewish people in the land of Israel at a time when Canaanite nations exist.

- P187 – Deuteronomy 7:2 – To destroy the seven Canaanite nations (The law of the seven nations)

---

[76] Numbered by Rambam. Grouped by applicability according to First Fruits of Zion.

CHAPTER 4

On the Heels of

"Ekev"
Deuteronomy 7:12–11:25

Ekev is the third reading from the book of Deuteronomy. The word *ekev* means "on the heels of" or "because of." Deuteronomy 7:12 says, "Then it shall come about, because you listen to these judgments and keep and do them, that the Lord your God will keep with you His covenant and His loving kindness which He swore to your forefathers." The word *ekev* shares the same root word as the name Jacob, who was born holding on to the heel of his twin brother. In this parsha, the word *ekev* is referencing the rewards that Israel will experience "on the heels of" keeping God's covenant and commandments.[77]

This portion not only examines the blessings for obedience (Deuteronomy 7:12–26) but also serves as a warning not to forget God in their prosperity. It is a mandate to remember. The Israelites had just spent forty years under the Lord's care as they were training in the wilderness (8:1–10). Moses warns them about the coming transition and reminds them to remember (8:11–20). Moses exposes the consequences of rebelling against God in verses 1–29. Moses recalled the second pair of tablets (10:1), the ark, Aaron's death, and the Levites' promotion (10:1–11). The essence of the law, and what God expects of His faithful, is reiterated in verses

---

[77] Boaz Michael. *Ekev* First Fruits of Zion. http://torahportions.org/this-portion. html?portion=Ekev (accessed May 20, 2014).

12–22. The parsha also details the rewards for obedience and the power of one's testimony (11:1–9), the good land (11:10–12), the Shema, part 2 (11:13–21), and conditional success (11:22–25).

To ensure success in their endeavor to enjoy the abundant blessings of the land God has promised, Moses continues to encourage the Israelites, stressing that all remnants of idolatry must be eliminated.[78] While God's love is unconditional, His blessings are not. Ekev carries the notion of reciprocity, of reward for obedience and punishment for disobedience. Verse 12 says, "If you pay attention …" the blessings are conditional and depend on their deliberate action. They will be blessed if they remember where they have been and from what they have been delivered. This is the covenant that the people of Israel have agreed to.

In this parsha, Moses also speaks of the seven species that are symbolic in the festival of Sukkot (8:8) as he reminds them not to forget lest they worship other gods. He reminds them that it is not of their own virtues that they receive this land but rather on the merit of their forefathers. The commandment of giving thanks after a meal is mentioned as well.

The Heels

Most commentaries on this parsha dwell on the words *ekev* or *eikev* and *eqev* found in the first verse. These are uncommon words for "because." Many commentators connect the word *eikev* with the word *akeuv*, as they are two Hebrew words with the same Hebrew spelling that are pronounced differently, but both mean "heel." Rashi interprets this as an allusion to a law, which people regard as relatively unimportant and so tend to tread on them with their heels.[79] Ibn Ezra would agree with Ramban that "the heels of" would represent the farther extremity of the body, in the sense that "in the end" the reward will follow the appropriate action.[80] According to Lubavitcher Rebbe, our commitment to the study of Torah should saturate our entire being, including the heel, the outermost, "lowest and

---

[78] Scherman. *Chumash*, 2000, 980.

[79] Scherman, Rashi. *Chumash*, 2000, 981.

[80] Chabad. *Parshat Eikev In-Depth*.http://www.chabad.org/parshah/in-depth/default_cdo/aid/53666/jewish/In-Depth.htm (accessed May 20, 2014).

least sensitive part of the person." He would insist that one should not only observe the laws on holy days or at certain holy hours but should embrace them in everyday activities.[81] In the same way that the heel is the base upon which the entire body stands and moves, Torah should be the driving force of daily living. As New Testament believers, we can choose to see the relevance in being absorbed in the Scripture as well. While there are many ways to learn, no learning method proves more effective than immersion study.

Remember the Wilderness

Remembering is the first key concept in this parsha. The Israelites' faith was strengthened upon this foundational concept. The first generation forgot the provisions that were made for them; how easy would it be for the next generation to forget? God assured the people they would have victory but that they would have to fight for it. According to Ramban, this was because if the Canaanites were not inhabiting the land right up to the moment the Israelites occupied it, wild beasts would populate it, and victory for the Israelites would come at an unacceptable cost.[82]

Boruch Leff argues one should appreciate the present and not always be focused on future reward.[83] This week, my granddaughter told me she just turned five years old, to which her little sister exclaimed, "I am almost four!" People everywhere are waiting to finish school or waiting to get married and have children. Almost immediately, those same people are waiting for their same children to grow up. A seventy-year-old cancer patient claimed to spend most of his life "dying" for these things to come, right until the point when he found himself just dying, and he discovered he had never really lived.[84] Much of my young adult years were filled with memories too painful to learn from. Many memories I struggled to forget. Yet the parsha of Ekev teaches that it is through the process that we learn the most. Moses did not want them to worry about the future or dwell on the mistakes or failures of their past. He beseeched the Israelites

---

[81] Ibid.

[82] Scherman, Rambam. *Chumash,* 2000, 981.

[83] Rabbi Boruch Leff. *Evek: Appreciating the Process.* http://www.aish.com/tp/i/ky/48959636.html (accessed May 20, 2014).

[84] Leff. *Ekev.* http://www.aish.com/tp/i/ky/48959636.html (accessed May 20, 2014).

to remember their past, to learn from their past, and to trust in God's provision to secure their future in the Promised Land. He wanted them to live in the here and now, where real freedom could be found. Proverbs 17:24 tells us a fool's eyes are directed to the ends of the earth. Rashi's thought was that a wise person thinks of the here and now with a focus on the process,[85] yet I still maintain, the focus must be on the eternal.

There were reasons for the Israelites' wilderness experience. It developed character. It gave them the opportunity to see God work miracles. It gave them a chance to prove and live out their faith. The hardships they experienced are no different from the hardship we can experience today. Without times of need, how can one appreciate the years of plenty? The Israelites are commanded to remember that nothing has come by their strength. This is where they are given the commandment to give thanks after meals. The idea is that God has already blessed everything in Genesis; all that is left is for us to bless God who gives the food. Remember the blessing, and then give thanks after it has been enjoyed. For most of us, we know where we are ultimately going, that is to heaven. Likewise, most of us remember where we started out, in some kind of captivity. Some spend more time oppressed by that captivity than others do; nevertheless, Christ has come to set us free! Everything else then, between our place of slavery and heaven, is a wilderness experience we are to remember.

Moses warned them about the blinding effects of prosperity. R'Matzlach believed prosperity could blind one to the identity of the source of the blessing.[86] This might call one to examine the meaning of prosperity. As some teachers today preach a prosperity gospel—be obedient and you will be rich—this would definitely take one's eye off the grace made possible through Christ and put the focus on works for salvation. Such a gospel could actually lead people into the dangerous territory of idolatry. Remember, Moses said, from whom the blessings and victories come. Remember the Exodus and the tribulations in the wilderness. Ramban believed that if they remembered, they would have to realize that it was not their strength, but God's, that enabled them to prevail.[87]

---

[85] Leff. Ekev. http://www.aish.com/tp/i/ky/48959636.html (accessed May 20, 2014).
[86] Scherman, R'Matzlach. *Chumash*, 2000, 984.
[87] Scherman, Rambam. *Chumash*, 2000, 985.

In chapter 8, Moses helps them remember their past disobedience. Here he lists some of the sins they committed after the Ten Commandments were given. This is to caution them to take their responsibilities seriously. Moses reminds them of their pattern of rebellion[88] and that their inheritance of the Promised Land was just that, an inheritance that was promised to their forefathers: Abraham, Isaac, and Jacob.

Remembering the unpleasant is also commanded. They are to "erase the memory of Amalek" (Deuteronomy 28:19) and "remember what Amalek did" (Deuteronomy 25:17), so it is customary for Jews to write the word *Amalek* and then cross it out.[89] Revelation 2:5 repeats, "Remember from where you have fallen, repent and do the deeds you did at first."

Expectations

Then what does God expect from humanity? The Torah assures the Israelites that if they are careful to observe all the commandments they can be certain that God will reward them with His covenant kindness. This obedience takes commitment on the part of humankind. Heschel reminds the reader that life without commitment is not worth living; our commitment is to be to God, and our roots are in the prophetic events of historical Israel.[90] The Torah makes it very clear what God expects: "to fear God, your God, to walk in all His ways, to love Him, to serve God, your God, with all your heart, and with all your soul, and to observe the commandments of God and His decrees" (10:12–13). Moses gives the Israelites this command for their benefit. The sages say there are two levels of God-fearing. The higher of the two is what Moses calls for here: a sense of awe and reverence. While it is easy for people to intellectually understand that one should feel this way about God, it is much harder for the ordinary person to achieve it. This is why Moses tells the people to cut away the barrier of their heart. Where the heart is the root of desire and emotion and as people sin habitually, the impulses for holiness become

---

[88] Scherman, Sforno. *Chumash,* 2000, 989.

[89] Reuven Brauner, *Laws of Kings and Wars: Translations from Rambam's Mishne Torah.* Raanana, Israel: Talmudic Books, 2012, 14.

[90] Abraham Joshua Heschel. *God in Search of Man: A Philosophy of Judaism.* New York: Farrar, Straus, and Giroux, 1983, 216.

weak. The Chumash describes it metaphorically: it is as if a covering that dulls spiritual perceptions surrounds the heart.[91]

Moses continues reminding the people whom they shall love. Just as God has loved the proselyte, so shall the Israelite. The Israelites were strangers in the land of Egypt and they, above all people, should have understood how it feels to be an outsider. God's love for the convert was great because he voluntarily accepted the Torah and thus the commandment to love the convert.[92]

Cleaving to God

Cleaving to God is a concept that the Talmud applies to the sages and Torah scholars of all generations. Citing Deuteronomy 10:20, the Talmud replies that for whoever attaches himself to a scholar, it is as if he has attached himself to God.[93] Rashi asks, "Is it possible to say such a thing? God is a 'consuming fire'! Therefore ' ... cleave to the dust of their [the scholars] feet, and drink thirstily their words."[94] In this case, I would disagree with the Talmud, as this Scripture is clear that the cleaving is to be to none other than God Himself. "You shall fear the Lord your God; you shall serve Him and cling (cleave) to Him, and you shall swear by His name" (Deuteronomy 10:20).

James reminds the Christians to draw near to God and He will draw near to them (4:8). Jesus' words are convicting as well. "If you love me, you will keep my commandments" (John 14:15). And the blessings, such as peace in daily living, wisdom, and fruit from our labor, will flow from our faithfulness.

It is important, however, for the scholar, teacher, and leader to be

---

[91] Scherman. *Chumash*, 2000, 991.

[92] Rambam, translated by Rabbi Berel Bell. *Sefer HaMitzvos of the Rambam Volume 1*, Kindle ed. Brooklyn: Sichos In English, 2013, 207. Kindle location 650.

[93] Samuel Daiches and Israel W. Slotki. *Soncino Babylonian Talmud Kethuboth*, Kindle ed. Teaneck, New Jersey: Talmudic Books, 2012, 111b. Kindle location 36869.

[94] Dovid Rosenfeld. *Chapter of Our Fathers*. Mishna, Pirkei Avos 1:4. Beit Shamesh, Israel. http://www.torah.org/learning/pirkei-avos/chapter1-4.html (accessed May 29, 2014).

continually aware that people are watching them, judging them, and making eternal decisions based on their behavior. It is equally important to note for the layman, the mother, and the teenager that they too are to be an example of one who cleaves to the one true God in all circumstances.

The Shema

The second section of the Shema (11:13–21) is covered in parsha Ekev. The Babylonian Talmud explains that this text, along with Deuteronomy 6:4–9, will be read morning and night. These two sections of the Shema are logically harmonious: the Shema being the acceptance of God's sovereignty and this second section being the acceptance of the yoke of the commandments.[95] This concept of reward and punishment is a primary concept in Judaism. Maimonides includes this concept in his Thirteen Principles of Faith. The implication is that God is aware of and concerned with all daily activities.[96]

Many of the commandments here involve action, and no explanation is needed as to the how-to in fulfilling this command. It is interesting to note, however, that when it comes to those commandments that involve emotion, Rambam feels compelled to map out the path toward achieving it. This is because emotions can't be commanded, but if one practices certain behavior, like pondering the great works of God, it will lead to the emotive part of loving and fearing God. Therefore, the commandments of the Torah spell out the exact path, and all one needs to do is embrace such a path. The process is what needs focus—not the results. When one is consistent in following such a path or process, the final goals of loving and fearing God will come.

The rabbis regarded the recitation of Shema as a form of Torah study; therefore, women were exempt from this law.[97] It was likely only the recitation of these Scriptures as they lie down and rise up to which they were exempt. The Talmud also notes that women were exempt from putting on

[95] Maurice Simon. *Soncino Babylonian Talmud: Berakoth,* Kindle ed. Teaneck, New Jersey: Talmudic Books, 2012, 13a. Kindle location 3153.

[96] Scherman, Rambam. *Chumash,* 2000, 995.

[97] David Weiss Halivni. *Midrash, Mishnah, and Gemara: The Jewish Predilection for Justified Law.* Cambridge, Massachusetts: Harvard University Press, 1986, 38–65.

the tefillin (phylacteries) but were still subject to the obligations of *tefillah* (prayer) mezuzah and saying grace after the meals.[98] The Talmud explains within this tractate that women are exempt from all positive time-related law. Women were exempt—not forbidden—because of the importance of their duties at home. According to our Jewish roots, "The woman is the cornerstone of the home, meaning the most important member of the household, whether individually or collectively."[99] This is not suggesting she is to be the spiritual leader in the home. It only emphasizes the importance of her work for the family unit. This begs a question: how did American society ever reach the point where the woman's role in the home was so menial that she needed to "come a long way, baby"? I would suggest it is the result of not remembering the wilderness experiences of our ancestors.

Humility

Remembering is to instill humility. Moses tells them to remember the entire path along which God has led them for the last forty years that they might know that they do not live by bread alone. Chapter 8 focuses on the humility of man. Moses knew that as their power and riches increased, they would be apt to follow other gods or believe their riches were a result of their own hard work. Moses knew this would be the greatest struggle of all time, even to this day.

According to a featured article on aish.com, the *Oxford English Dictionary* announced that the word *selfie* was the International Word of the Year for 2013.[100] A selfie is a self-portrait taken with a smartphone. The article notes that more than fifty-three million selfies were uploaded in 2013 to social media platforms like Facebook. They noted a site that featured "funeral selfies" and elected the winner of the "Selfie Hall of

---

[98] Maurice Simon. *Soncino Babylonian Talmud: Berakoth*, Kindle ed. Teaneck, New Jersey: Talmudic Books, 2012, 20a–20b. Kindle location 3153.

[99] Rabbi Menachem Mendel Schneerson, translated by Chassida Halevi. *Good Advice: 50 Suggestions for a Good Life, Jewish Wisdom Collection*. Israel: Ruach Nachon Publishing House, Kindle edition. Kindle location 168.

[100] Rabbi Benjamin Blech. *Selfies: The Word of the Year*. http://www.aish.com/ci/s/Selfies-The-Word-of-the-Year.html (accessed December 17, 2013).

Fame," taken December 2013 by the president of the United States, Barack Obama, British Prime Minister David Cameron, and Danish Prime Minister Helle Thorning-Schmidt at the memorial service for former South African President Nelson Mandela. The selfie is a display of the worst kind of idolatry: pride. It seems all folly boils down to this one thing: pride. In this day of the iPhone, iPad, and iPod, the selfie describes more than something people are doing; it describes an international obsession. "I can do it myself because it's all about me." This attitude is destruction and bondage waiting to happen.

The largest problem with a self-focused attitude is in the power of the Enemy when the trials of life rain down on one's dreams. If Job had been self-focused, he would have been looking for a new god long before God really blessed him. A self-focused view of life thinks, *What can I get out of this?* or *What can God do for me?* A kingdom-focused life will humbly realize who has the best plan. This attitude would be in a continual search for ways to bless the Lord. This individual's prayer might be "What can I do for You, God?" When this person faces cancer, a wheelchair, or another calamity, his or her prayer might sound more like "Please use me for Your kingdom purpose." Consequently, the circumstances are not as oppressive as they can be for the self-focused individual.

At times, it takes great humility to admit we need help with even the smallest of daily activities. This is especially true when one's field, bank account, and belly are full. Aristotle writes much on humility, saying that when others are humble, all feel calm when in their presence and anger ceases.[101]

Here in Deuteronomy 8, we find the directive of saying grace after meals. Deuteronomy 8:10 commands, "When you have eaten and are satisfied, you shall bless the LORD your God for the good land which He has given you." This order applies whenever one eats a meal with bread and is satisfied.[102] This is a display of humility as one remembers that all things come from God: the manna that falls from the sky, the rain that falls from

---

[101] Aristotle. *Rhetoric*, translated by W. Rhys Roberts. Publish This, LLC, 2007. Kindle location 38535.
[102] Maurice Simon. *Soncino Babylonian Talmud: Berakoth*, Kindle ed. Teaneck, New Jersey: Talmudic Books, 2012, 48b. Kindle location 10420.

sky, and the food we buy in the store today. It is easy to be thankful when one sits before a table of food with an empty stomach. The difficult part is maintaining that attitude of gratitude when the stomach is satisfied.

Isaiah 49:14–51:3 is the second Haftarah of Consolation. The parsha begins as follows: "'God has forsaken me,' Zion sighs, 'my Sovereign has forgotten me'" (49:14). While this first verse does not offer much consolation, the rest of the parsha responds with a positive and hopeful promise of future redemption. Isaiah the prophet reminds the people of the rebellion that brought on their exile. He also describes a time when the Israelites will return to the land that God had promised their forefathers. Knowing that the Jewish people felt abandoned by God, Isaiah then tells the people to remember the promises made to Abraham and Sarah and to remember and look forward to the greatest blessing God has for them: the arrival of Messiah. Isaiah continues through the Haftarah to use metaphors to describe the Israelites' return and how the nations of the world will help. He talks about marriage and notes that the Jewish people and God are like two people in a personal and powerful relationship. The Haftarah concludes with the inspiring words of Isaiah. "For God shall comfort Zion, He shall comfort all her ruins … joy, and gladness shall be found there, thanksgiving and the sound of music" (51:3).

The New Testament speaks of humility as well. True humility is recognized in the tax collector who had nothing and stood at the bottom of a hill, unwilling to lift his eyes to heaven (Luke 18:9–14). The Christian is to walk in a manner worthy of his or her calling with humility and gentleness (Ephesians 4:2), doing nothing from selfish conceit (Philippians 2:3) but rather putting on a heart of compassion, kindness, humility, gentleness, and patience, forgiving each other just as Jesus forgives (Colossians 3:12).

Listen

If you listen, you will be blessed; if you do not, you will suffer the consequences. The choice is yours. This parsha demonstrates that it is easy to see how remembering past failures, past pain, and past tragedy can help illuminate one's dependence on the one true God. No one can do it by himself or herself, although many believe they can, at least until they fail. Ekev teaches us about the power of a testimony, the power in the experience. While something may have been very painful or humiliating, the firsthand testimony of that experience can bring many to a saving faith. The Chumash tells us that Moses stressed the personal involvement of his listeners, claiming it is incumbent upon everyone to use his own experience to deepen his love for God and set an example for his students.[103] This will also bring others to faith in the finished work of Jesus. Psalm 107:2 reminds the redeemed of the Lord to speak out. On (ekev) the heels of, or after, any experience, "Let the redeemed of the Lord say so" (Psalm 107:2). The apostle Paul wrote about his testimony repeatedly (Acts 9:21–23; 22:5–7; 26:11–13; 26:19–21), and people continue to this day to listen to his story. The Israelites' experience and testimony are what we read about in the Torah. After those experiences, many came to worship God in the Promised Land. It is because of those testimonies penned in the Torah, Haftarah, and Brit Chadasha that many today are still being added to the kingdom of God. It is on (ekev) the heels of a testimony that God commands each of His children today to write it down and pass it on.

Mitzvot[104]

All mitzvah this week apply to the Jewish people and God-fearing Gentile believers in every time and place, including the Christian.

- N22 – Deuteronomy 7:25 – Not benefiting from ornaments which have adorned an idol
- N25 – Deuteronomy 7:26 – Not increasing wealth from anything connected with idolatry
- P19 – Deuteronomy 8:10 – Saying grace after meals
- P207 – Deuteronomy 10:19 – Loving a stranger, convert, proselyte
- P4 – Deuteronomy 10:20 – Fearing God
- P6 – Deuteronomy 10:20 – Cleaving to God
- P5 – Deuteronomy 11:10 – Serving God
- P7 – Deuteronomy 10:20 – Swearing only by God's name

---

[103] Scherman. *Chumash*, 2000, 993.

[104] Numbered by Rambam. Grouped by applicability according to First Fruits of Zion.

CHAPTER 5

See

"Re'eh"
Deuteronomy 11:26–16:17

In Re'eh, the forty-seventh parsha, we see a shift in the focus from the basic beliefs of Judaism to specific duties of the Jew. After Moses reminds the people of the blessing if they obey and the curses if they do not obey, he reviews the laws of the sacrifices, idolatry, *kashrut*, charity, the sabbatical year, slavery, and the festivals.

The name given to this parsha *Re'eh* means to "see." "See, I am setting before you a blessing (beracha) and a curse (kelalah)" (Deuteronomy 11:26). Moses commands the Israelites to place certain blessings on Mount Gerizim and certain curses on Mount Ebal. Parsha Ki Tavo describes the exact procedure for this ceremony (Deuteronomy 27:11).

The doctrine of free will is a fundamental principle to the Jew. "Though everything is foreseen by God, yet free will is granted to humanity."[105] The majority of the commandments in Deuteronomy are in Re'eh and the next two parashot. There are fifty-six mitzvot in Re'eh alone.

Starting in Re'eh, Moses simplifies the 613 commands as a choice between blessing and curse. Malbim claims this is more than a simple promise, as the sense of accomplishment, fulfillment, and spiritual growth

---

[105] Dovid Rosenfeld. *Can Man Destroy the World?* Mishna Avot 3.19(a). http://www.torah.org/learning/pirkei-avos/chapter3-19a.html (2009) (accessed May 20, 2014).

can be seen in those who are Torah observant.[106] This parsha highlights some of the key concepts of the Torah-observant Jew.

Mutual Responsibility

The concept of arevut has to do with one's responsibility for others. For the Jew, this mutual responsibility is not merely a concern for other Jews, but for the Gentile as well. In the same way as one who cosigns on a financial loan is responsible to repay the debt, so is one always responsible for another's life. The concept of arevut extends to the obligations of the law as well. For example, it is a law to blow the shofar (a ram's horn) on 10 Tishrei in the jubilee year (Leviticus 25:9).[107] One person can blow the shofar for the entire congregation. The only caveat to arevut is that one cannot perform a legal obligation for another that he himself is not obligated to uphold. This means that a woman could not blow the shofar for the congregation because the law does not apply to her.[108] Rebbe argues that responsibility is a basic human need, like food or oxygen, and that one cannot live in freedom without it.[109] No doubt, Jesus had the concept of arevut in mind when He told the story about the Good Samaritan to articulate the kind of mercy that is expected of His followers (Luke 10:37) or when He chose to accept responsibility for mankind's sin and die on the cross.

For the Christian, arevut would also mean having a burden for the lost. One doesn't need to be a pastor or an elder to share the love of Jesus and the truth of salvation with one person at a time. Any Christian can reach out to others who do not understand the freedom given to them by Christ. We can go door to door with the message of salvation or simple leave a gospel track with a generous tip at a restaurant. Edmund Burke

---

[106] Jewish Virtual Library: http://www.jewishvirtuallibrary.org/jsource/judaica/ejud_0002_0013_0_13087.html (accessed May 16, 2014).

[107] Ronald L. Eisenberg. *The 613 Mitzvot,* Kindle ed. Shengold Publishers, Schreiber Publishing, 2012. Kindle location 6817.

[108] Naftali Brawer. *A Brief Guide to Judaism: Theology, History, and Practice,* Kindle ed. London: Robinson, 2013. Kindle location 1351.

[109] Simon Jacobson. Toward a Meaningful Life, New Edition: The Wisdom of the Rebbe Menachem Mendel Schneerson, Kindle ed. HarperCollins, 2010. Kindle location 2771.

said, "The only thing necessary for the triumph of evil is for good men to do nothing." Was it merely a coincidence that I heard Burke's quote as I silently pondered all the reasons why I should not or could not publish this book? I had to question, "Would I be 'doing nothing' if I ignore the tug to speak out?" Heaven forbid I be part of the silent majority and let evil triumph without a fight! Jesus' death on the cross is a shining example of arevut, one all Christians should consider when speaking up seems like too much work.

Idolatry

Arevut is a foundational value in Judaism. It extends from the responsibility to serve and protect to the concept of rebuking others and holding them accountable so they might live a righteous life. This idea, called *tochachah* (correction),[110] comes from Leviticus 19:17. "You shall not hate your fellow countryman in your heart; you may surely reprove your neighbor, but shall not incur sin because of him." Rabbi Simeon said, "If you carry out the judgment against the apostate city it is as if you offered up a burnt-offering whole before me."[111] The command "to destroy all idols and their place of worship" includes breaking, burning, and dismantling any shrine or temple used for idol worship. This commandment applies to the Jew in the land of Israel. As Deuteronomy 12:1 states, "You shall carefully observe in the land ..."

According to Rashi, idolatry is a rejection of God because one who worships an idol has essentially repudiated the entire Torah.[112] This is why simply tearing down the asherah pole is not enough. The Jew is to burn it and dig up its roots. The only way to avoid sin is to remove all temptation. The Israelites were not even to refer to the idols by their proper names, but rather they were to use a derogatory name for them.

The rabbis determined that there were seven basic laws that were

[110] Gary O. Aidekman is president of United Jewish Communities of MetroWest New Jersey. *http://ljfedgmw.org/page.aspx?id=237417* (accessed January 2, 2014).
[111] Isaac Sassoon and Isaac D. D. Sassoon. Destination Torah: Notes and Reflections on Selected Verses from the Weekly Torah Readings. Jersey City: Ktav Pub, Inc., 2001, 285.
[112] Scherman, Rashi. *Chumash*, 2000, 999.

binding on all humans in the entire world. These seven laws, referred to as the Noahide Laws, were imperative to establishing a civilized society. Included in these seven were adultery, murder, and idolatry.[113]

The ancient idolaters believed that with enough worship to the right idol, they could bring rain in the dry seasons and fertility to the barren womb, as if they had control over such things. In much the same way, some people today obsess over things referred to as hobbies or even responsibilities to feel like they have control over them. Anything can become an idol as one tries to gain control. Even worship can become a form of idolatry, as can be seen in the behavior of the Pharisees. According to Eisenberg, the only thing that has changed in the last two thousand years is the level of sophistication used by the contemporary man.[114] The rabbis believed that some commandments, like the preservation of life, were so important that even if it meant forsaking another command, they were to be kept. However, the seven Noahide commands were never to be broken, even if it meant death. Idolatry, adultery, and murder were absolutely forbidden. In other words, it was forbidden to save one man's life if it meant killing another. To die for this belief was to commit the holiest act of all. This was known as *kiddush hashem* (kiddush = holy; hashen = the name).[115] The other commands included in the Noahide Law were the establishment of courts of justice and the prohibition of blasphemy, incest, robbery, and eating flesh cut from a live animal (before it is killed).

Kosher Laws

Kosher Laws, known as Kashrut, refers to the dietary laws. These laws explain which animals are clean and unclean. The list of the kosher animals distinguishes the clean from the unclean by their hooves and their cud-chewing behavior. The scales on the fish differentiate the water creatures. Also mentioned here is permission to sell any unclean carcass to the stranger or foreigner. There was a vivid distinction between clean and unclean. The rabbis argue for more meaning than just what one puts into

---

[113] Eisenberg. *The 613 Mitzvot,* 2012. Kindle location 373.

[114] Brawer. *A Brief Guide to Judaism,* 2013. Kindle location 1835.

[115] Ibid. Kindle location 2158.

the mouth. It would include separating the holy from the unholy even to the point of distinguishing between holy and less holy. Prayers of separation (*habdalah*) are said any time the shofar is not blown.[116] This law is echoed in 2 Corinthians 6:17. Paul urges his listeners to separate themselves from the unclean. The apostle Paul writes of this concept when he explains that a little leaven leavens the lump (1 Corinthians 5:6; Galatians 5:9). In contrast, the Christian can be assured that nothing can separate him or her from the love of God (Romans 8:38).

Be Strong

The prohibition against eating blood appears no less than seven times in the Torah.[117] There are many views on this command. Rabbi Yehudah claims, "The words of Scripture are to be interpreted exactly as written."[118] Tradition taught that eating the blood was a common practice for the Israelite. According to Rambam, the Jewish people learned to eat blood in Egypt as an idolatrous ceremony[119] forty years before the text of Deuteronomy took place, yet Moses felt it necessary to once again stress the importance of being strong and not eating blood. Rashi, on the other hand, felt this came only as a caution to teach the importance of observing the law. He claimed that if one is cautioned against eating the blood, which no one really wants to do, how much more important is it that one remain strong to keep all the other commands that prohibit one from doing things that are pleasurable to the senses?[120]

Ephesians 6 reminds the Christian to put on the whole armor of God. Most interpret this to mean daily, as one rises, one girds one's loins. Then with shoes of peace, shield of faith, helmet of salvation, and the Word

---

[116] Tzvee Zahavy. *Kosher Talmud: Babylonian Talmud Hullin,* Kindle ed. Talmudic Books, 2012. Kindle location 2617.

[117] Rambam. *Sefer Hamitzvos,* Shoresh 9 cited on http://www.chabad.org/parshah/article_cdo/aid/704636/jewish/Be-Strong.htm (accessed May 29, 2014).

[118] H. Freedman. *Soncino Babylonian Talmud Pesahim,* Kindle ed. Teaneck, New Jersey: Talmudic Books. 21b, 2012. Kindle location 3009.

[119] Rambam, Moses Maimonides. *Guide for the Perplexed—Enhanced Version Christian Classics,* Kindle ed. Ethereal Library, 2009. Kindle location 11120.

[120] Scherman, Rashi. *Chumash,* 2000, 1005.

of God, the Christian is strong. I would take that one step farther and interpret this to mean one should never take the armor off.

Harris extrapolates from the Talmud.[121] "Four things require fortitude in the observance: The law, good works, prayer, and social duties." Harris notes that the Talmud quotes Joshua 1:7 with respect to the law and good works, claiming that the word "strong" refers to law and "firm" refers to good works. With respect to prayer, the Talmud quotes Psalm 27:14. "Wait for the Lord; be strong, and let your heart take courage; Yes, wait for the Lord." Finally, 2 Samuel 10:12 can be seen in the Talmud: "Be strong, and let us show ourselves courageous for the sake of our people and for the cities of our God."[122] We find this repeated in the Chumash at the end of every book of the Torah. At the completion of each book, the Jew will recite, "Chazak! Chazak! Venitchazeik!" "Be strong! Be strong! And may we be strengthened!"

Types of Tithes

Three types of tithes are discussed in Re'eh. Ten percent of one's produce was to go to the Levite. This was because the Levite did not have a share in the land. This type of tithe was called *ma'aser rishon*. Another tenth of the harvest of the land was taken to the appointed place and eaten in celebration. This was called the *ma'aser sheni* and was observed in the first, second, fourth, and fifth years of the sabbatical cycle *(shemittah)*. In the third and sixth years of the shemittah, *ma'aser ani* (another 10 percent) was given to the poor who were also allowed to glean from the crops.

The practice of tithing is carried forward into the New Testament as Paul tells us all will reap what they sow and no one should give grudgingly or under compulsion, for God loves a cheerful giver (2 Corinthians 9:6–8).

---

[121] Simon. *Berakoth*, 2012. Kindle location 7373.

[122] Maurice Harris. Hebraic Literature: Translations from the Talmud, Midrashim, and Kabbala, Kindle ed. New York: Tudor Publishing Company, 2012, 1008.

The Sabbatical Year

The Sabbatical Year is known in Hebrew as *shemittah*. Deuteronomy 15:1–4 repeats the three commands given in Leviticus 25. First, cancel monetary claims in the sabbatical year. "At the end of every seven years you shall grant a remission of debts." Second, exact debts from idolaters or foreigners. "From a foreigner you may exact it ... but your hand shall release whatever of yours is with your brother." Third, do not demand payment of debts after the shemittah year. "This is the manner of remission: every creditor shall release what he has loaned to his neighbor; he shall not exact it of his neighbor and his brother, because the LORD's remission has been proclaimed." During this year, creditors must forgive outstanding loans to fellow Jews. The requirement is to help the poor as long as they need it, freely and without judgment. The compound verb indicates to give and then give again (Rashi).

This is a time of rest for the land. During the shemittah, it was forbidden to cultivate the soil, prune the trees, or reap anything that grows by itself. It was prohibited for people to treat their fields as their own and prevent others from enjoying the harvest. The produce could be eaten by everyone (owners, Gentile laborers, and wild animals alike), and used exclusively for food (not commerce).[123] As the need for Jews to grow food in Israel became an acute issue in modern times, the observance of the sabbatical year became a problem. To cope with this situation, most rabbinic authorities permitted Jewish farmers to sell their land to non-Jews for the shemittah period. In this way, they could cultivate the land as nonowners.[124]

It was also forbidden to gather fruit in the same way as one would normally gather. For example, grapes were normally trodden in a wine press, but this was forbidden. One could use a vat or other bucket not normally used.[125]

---

[123] Eisenberg. *The 613 Mitzvot,* 2012. Kindle location 5445.

[124] Ibid. Kindle location 5448.

[125] Eisenberg. *The 613 Mitzvot,* 2012. Kindle location 5440.

After the shemittah year had passed, a Jew could not ask for repayment of a loan from another Jew, although this did not apply to the foreigner. In Deuteronomy 15, Moses also warns against being stingy because the shemittah year was near. This was intended to create a dignified people who genuinely cared for each other. Hillel recognized the harmful consequences of shemittah year and introduced the Prosbul. The Prosbul allowed for collection of a loan after the shemittah years. This was beneficial to both the rich and the poor as it protected the rich, their property, and their right to repayment while the poor could still get a loan if needed in the fifth and sixth years of the shemittah cycle.[126]

Appointed Places

The parsha of Emor lists eight main mo'edim, or "the appointed times," of the Lord in Scripture. This parsha of Re'eh discusses those appointed places. Idolatry was on the rampage. Because it was a common practice in Canaan to worship false gods to the point of sacrificing children, the people were commanded to destroy all statues and objects related to idolatry. They were forbidden to serve in any way that even resembled a pagan ritual, so the Lord commanded them to worship Him only in the appointed places. In 12:21, we see a caveat is given. "If the place the Lord, your God, chooses to put His Name there, will be distant from you, you may slaughter of your cattle and of your sheep, which the Lord has given you, as I have commanded you, and you may eat in your cities, according to every desire of your soul."[127]

The Westminster Confession of Faith (19:3–5) states that while the sundry judicial laws and ceremonial laws have been abolished under the New Testament, the moral laws will bind forever and in fact are strengthened by the New Testament. Luther and Schreiner would argue, however, that the Law in its entirety has been abrogated by the atoning death of

---

[126] Sha'are Bloch. http://www.jewishencyclopedia.com/articles/12390-prosbul (accessed May 20, 2014).
[127] Scherman, Rashi. *Chumash*, 2000, 1004.

Jesus,[128] including the requirement to keep the appointed feast, festivals, and even the Sabbath,[129] which seems consistent with Colossians 2:16–17. This begs a question: if the Law does not bind, does that mean it should be abandoned completely? Because we could not or would not be caught committing a crime, should we? I think the apostle Paul would concur, as he believed that the Christian no longer needed to conform to the law to be saved, yet he was vehemently opposed to the idea of lawless living (Romans 3:31, 6). Most churches today do not teach of the feasts or the mo'edim, dismissing them as completely irrelevant. Special services celebrate Christmas and Easter in most Christian churches while encouraging the traditional meal, yet Passover and Sukkot go unnoticed. Messer argues that the mo'edim contain blessings that bring glory to God that cannot be obtained without regard to God's teaching and instruction on the Torah.[130]

Hebrews 10:24–25 reiterates the need to keep the mo'edim. "Let us consider how to stimulate one another to love and good deeds, not forsaking our own assembling together." Keeping the appointed times is the peace offering (voluntary offering) the Christian can still give; an offering of thanksgiving, praise, and worship through the communion of the saints and the breaking of bread.[131] Whether the Christian celebrates the Sabbath or Sunday, Passover or Easter, Sukkot or Christmas, the focus needs to be on the reason for the celebration, not the festival itself.

Three Yearly Feasts

After encouraging the people to bring their second tithes to Jerusalem, the Torah now speaks of the three pilgrimage festivals known as *shelosh regalim*. In addition to the law regarding attendance at each of these holidays,

---

[128] Martin Luther. *How Christians Should Regard Moses,* Luther Works, vol. 35, *Word and Sacrament,* ed. Helmut T. Lehmann (general editor) and E. Theodore Bachman. Philadelphia: Muhlenberg Press, 1960, 161.

[129] Schreiner and Merkle. *40 Questions,* 2010, 91.

[130] Rabbi Ralph Messer. *Torah: Law or Grace?* "Kingdom Principles for Kingdom Living," Kindle ed. STBM Publishing, 2011. Kindle location 536.

[131] Robert F Kingscote, *Christ as Seen in the Offerings,* Kindle ed. Bible Truth Publishers, 2011. Kindle location 516.

we find some detail on behavior during these festivals as being a joyous and celebratory time. The three festivals are Passover, Shavu'ot, and Sukkot. All Jewish men are required to attend the holy temple during these holidays.

Passover

Passover, or Pesach, also known as the Festival of Redemption, is the first of the three yearly festivals. Agriculturally, Passover represents the beginning of the harvest season. It is also a celebration of freedom from the bondage of the Egyptians.[132] It is celebrated with a seder meal, and all foods and Scripture read during the meal are to be a reminder of the Israelites' freedom from oppression. Matzo is an unleavened bread commonly eaten by the Jew during this seven-day holiday (eight days if living outside of Israel). The matzo is a reminder of the affliction the Israelites had to endure and how they had to leave Egypt in haste.

The Feast of Weeks

Shavu'ot is Hebrew for "weeks," also known as "shavu'ot" or "The Festival of First Fruits." Shavu'ot is celebrated on 6 Sivan by most Jews,[133] seven weeks after Passover. Agriculturally, Shavu'ot celebrates the day when the firstfruits were harvested and brought to the temple. The Old Testament gives no historical meaning to Shavu'ot. The Mishna and Talmud, however, say the feast celebrates the giving of the Torah at Mount Sinai,[134] also known as *Hag Matan Torateinu* (the Festival of the Giving of Our Torah).[135] While Passover created a physical freedom from bondage, the giving of the Torah on Shavu'ot was a freedom for the soul and spirit from the bondage to idolatry and immorality. The Christian also knows Shavu'ot as Pentecost because it also falls on the fiftieth day after Passover; Shavu'ot has no particular similarity to the Christian holiday of Pentecost.

---

[132] History and Overview. http://www.jewishvirtuallibrary.org/jsource/Judaism/holidaya.html (accessed May 20, 2014).

[133] William Mark Huey. *Counting the Omer: A Daily Devotional toward Shavu'ot,* Kindle ed. Richardson: TNN Press, 2011. Kindle location 213.

[134] Karesh and Hurvitz. *Encyclopedia of Judaism,* 2006. Kindle location 9962.

[135] Huey. *Counting the Omer,* 2011. Kindle location 91.

Unlike the other two festivals, Shavu'ot does not have many requirements. The primary instructions are found in Leviticus 23 and Deuteronomy 16.[136] Shavu'ot lasts a single day.[137] It is customary to stay up all night of Shavu'ot and study Torah. In the morning, as early as possible, they pray and light *yahrzeit* candles.[138] Mock wedding ceremonies are held to symbolize the marriage covenant between God and Israel. Feasting on dairy and triangular foods is also traditional.[139]

Some Christians celebrate Shavu'ot as they remember the coming of the Holy Spirit. Shavu'ot, also known as "Pentecost," comes from the Greek *Pentekoste*, meaning "fiftieth." Messianic Jews celebrate the giving of the Torah and the giving of the Spirit.[140]

Other notable activities on Shavu'ot include confirmation ceremonies,[141] Hallel prayers, the reading of the book of Ruth, and remembrance of loved ones who have passed on.

It is with great anticipation that the Jews count the omer to Shavu'ot. On this day, they are to remember the terrible tragedies and plagues they have endured as well, but their love for the Word of God exceeds all else.

The Feast of Tabernacles

The Feast of Tabernacles is the third of the pilgrimage festivals, and it lasts seven days. The Feast of Tabernacles is also known as the Feast of Booths, the Feast of the Ingathering, or in Hebrew, *Sukkot*. It is at the end of the harvest, and it is intended as a reminder of the frail huts that the Israelites lived in for their forty years as they wandered through the desert. Sukkot comes four days after Yom Kippur.[142]

The first record we have of Jesus attending one of these feasts according to the custom of the Jews in which He was raised is found in Luke 2:24 when He was twelve years old. In John 7:8–10, we read that Jesus

---

[136] Huey. *Counting the Omer*, 2011. Kindle location 162.

[137] Karesh and Hurvitz. *Encyclopedia of Judaism*, 2006. Kindle location 9958.

[138] Ibid. Kindle location 11750.

[139] Ibid. Kindle location 9967.

[140] Huey. *Counting the Omer*, 2011. Kindle location 630.

[141] Karesh and Hurvitz. *Encyclopedia of Judaism*, 2006. Kindle location 2418.

[142] Brawer. *A Brief Guide to Judaism*, 2013. Kindle location 3407.

celebrated Sukkot and encouraged His disciples to do the same. In 1 Corinthians 5:8, the Scripture insists that one should celebrate the feast for Christ, the true Passover, has been sacrificed. Nowhere in the New Testament does it specifically say that those who follow the way of Jesus should ignore these *shelosh regalim*. We do, however, read in Colossians 2 that we are not to judge those who don't. More detail on Yom Kippur and Sukkot is included later in chapter 11.

Listen Carefully

Deuteronomy 32:46 repeats, "Take to your heart all the words with which I am warning you today which you shall command your sons to observe carefully, even all the words of this law." The Haftarah portion read with Re'eh (Isaiah 54:11–55:5) is the third Haftarah of Consolation and offers encouragement to the Jew. At this time in history, Jerusalem was destroyed and laid to waste. The text reveals that the Lord will prevail and will lay their foundation in sapphires, walls of rubies, and gates of crystal, and all will be taught of the Lord. The stipulation is set forth in the second half of the Haftarah that the people must turn to Him, listen carefully, eat what is good, delight in abundance, and be far from oppression. Verse 3 repeats this stipulation. "Incline your ear, and come to Me. Listen that you may live; And I will make an everlasting covenant with you, according to the faithful mercies shown to David." Jesus Christ repeated this. Some will argue that the entire life of Jesus is one argument after another as to why we should listen.[143] Heidebrecht points out that hearing God's voice starts with listening. He recognizes eight ways that God speaks to mankind today, including through the Scripture (2 Timothy 3:16), creation (Psalms 19:1–2), the Holy Spirit (John 14:26), other people (Romans 10:17), difficulties (Psalm 119:67–68), circumstances (Romans 8:28), angels (Hebrews 1:14), and blessings (James 1:17).[144]

"All authority has been given to Me in heaven and on earth. Go therefore and make disciples of all the nations, baptizing them in the name of

---

[143] John Piper. *What Jesus Demands from the World*. Wheaton: Crossway Books, 2006, 56.

[144] Vern Heidebrecht. *Hearing God's Voice: Eight Keys to Connecting with God,* Kindle ed. Colorado Springs: David C Cook, 2010, 1367.

the Father and the Son and the Holy Spirit, teaching them to observe all that I commanded you; and lo, I am with you always, even to the end of the age" (Matthew 28:18–20). Clearly, the concept of arevut is repeated here in the New Testament as the command is to all disciples, all Christians, men and women. Teach them, the text says, "all that I commanded you." The implication here is that the New Testament believers are responsible to teach and care for the Jew and the Gentile.

The US Declaration of Independence recognizes that "all men are created equal and endowed by their Creator with certain unalienable Rights."[145] Equality is also a Jewish value. The Torah tells us that we are all created in the image of God and that we all have divine attributes and certain rights simply by virtue of being human. If that is true, then we are equally responsible for the spiritual health of our fellow Christians as well as the pagans or heathen among us. If all Christians were to take the concept of arevut seriously, as Jesus certainly did when He chose to bear the burden of our sin on the cross, then all nations would find the true freedom found only in salvation, and truth would reign.

Mitzvot[146]

Applies to everyone in every place and time.

- N171 – Deuteronomy 14:1 – Not tearing out hair for the dead
- N45 – Deuteronomy 14:1 – Not cutting in our flesh
- N182 – Deuteronomy 12:23 – Not eating a limb or any part (blood) of a living animal
- N28 – Deuteronomy 13:3 – Not listening to or paying attention to the prophesy or prophet made in the name of an idol
- N313 – Deuteronomy 12:32 – Not adding to the written or oral law
- N314 – Deuteronomy 12:32 – Not detracting from the written or oral Law

---

[145] The Declaration of Independence. http://www.ushistory.org/Declaration/document/ (accessed May 20, 2014).

[146] Numbered by Rambam. Grouped by applicability according to First Fruits of Zion.

Applies to the Jew and God-fearing Gentiles in every time and place.

- P146 – Deuteronomy 12:21 – Slaughtering animals before eating them
- N16 – Deuteronomy 13:12 – Not trying to persuade an Israelite to worship idols; not being an enticer
- P150 – Deuteronomy 14:11 – Searching for the prescribed signs in birds
- N180 – Deuteronomy 14:21 – Not eating the meat of an animal that has died of itself *(nevelah)*
- N181 – Deuteronomy 14:21 – Not eating the meat of a torn animal *(tereah)*
- N140 – Deuteronomy 14:3 – Not eating the invalidated consecrated offerings (animals that have become blemished after slaughter)
- N113 – Deuteronomy 15:19 – Not doing any work with a dedicated (consecrated) beast
- N114 – Deuteronomy 15:19 – Not shearing a dedicated beast
- N232 – Deuteronomy 15:7 – Not failing to give charity to our needy brethren
- P195 – Deuteronomy 15:8 – Giving charity
- N231 – Deuteronomy 15:9 – Not withholding a loan to be canceled by the Shemittah year
- N65 – Deuteronomy 12:4 – Not breaking down houses of worship or to destroy holy books

Applies to the Jew and God-fearing Gentiles with the temple and Levitical system in place.

- N148 – Deuteronomy 12:17, 18 – Not eating the firstfruits offerings before they are set down in the sanctuary grounds
- N89 – Deuteronomy 12:13 – Not offering sacrifices outside the temple court
- P84 – Deuteronomy 12:14 – Bringing all offering to the sanctuary; not offering them outside the temple

- N147 – Deuteronomy 12:15 – Not eating offerings of lesser holiness before the priests apply their blood to the altar
- N144 – Deuteronomy 12:17 – Not eating an unblemished firstling outside Jerusalem
- N145 – Deuteronomy 12:17 – Not eating an unblemished firstling outside Jerusalem
- N146 – Deuteronomy 12:17 – Not eating the meat of a burnt offering

Applies to judges in a court of law, both Jews and Gentiles, in every time and place.

- P719 – Deuteronomy 13:14 – Inquiring into the testimony of witnesses, to examine witnesses thoroughly

Applies to Jewish and God-fearing slave owners in every place during the years when the jubilee is observed.

- N233 – Deuteronomy 15:13 – Not sending a Hebrew bondman away empty-handed
- P196 – Deuteronomy 15:14 – Lavishing gifts on the Hebrew slave when he is freed
- P128 – Deuteronomy 14:22 – Setting aside the second tithe
- P130 – Deuteronomy 14:28 – Setting aside the poor man's tithe in the third and sixth year

Applies to Jewish lenders and God-fearing Gentile believers only when the laws of the jubilee year are observed, but by rabbinic extension, in every time and place.

- P141 – Deuteronomy 15:3 – Canceling monetary claims in the Sabbatical year
- P142 – Deuteronomy 15:3 – Exacting debts from idolaters or a foreigner
- N230 – Deuteronomy 15:2 – Not demanding payment of debts after Shemittah year

Applies to Jewish livestock owners with the temple and Levitical system in place.

- P86 – Deuteronomy 12:15 – Redeeming sanctified animals that develop a blemish

Applies to Jewish males in the land of Israel with the temple and Levitical system in place.

- P53 – Deuteronomy 16:16 – Appearing before the Lord during the festivals
- N156 – Deuteronomy 16:16 – Not appearing in sanctuary on festival without sacrifice

Applies to Jewish people doing agriculture in the land of Israel with the temple and Levitical system in place.

- N141 – Deuteronomy 12:17 – Not eating unredeemed the second tithe of grain outside of Jerusalem
- N142 – Deuteronomy 12:17 – Not consuming the second tithe of wine outside of Jerusalem
- N143 – Deuteronomy 12:17 – Not consuming the second tithe of oil outside of Jerusalem.

Applies to Jews in every place and time.

- P54 – Deuteronomy 16:14 – Rejoicing or being joyful during the festivals
- N17 – Deuteronomy 13:9 – Not loving someone who seeks to mislead you to idols; not to love an enticer
- N19 – Deuteronomy 13:9 – Not saving the life of a misleader\ enticer
- N20 – Deuteronomy 13:9 – Not pleading for the misleader\enticer
- N21 – Deuteronomy 13:9 – Not oppressing evidence unfavorable to the misleader\enticer; not refraining from speaking against an enticer

- N175 – Deuteronomy 14:19 – Not eating any swarming winged insect
- N199 – Deuteronomy 16:3 – Not eating chometz after noon of 14 Nissan
- N18 – Deuteronomy 13:9 – Not relaxing one's hatred toward an enticer

Applies to Jewish people in Jerusalem with the temple and Levitical system in place.

- N118 – Deuteronomy 16:4 – Not allowing meat of 14 Nissan Festival Offering *(chagigah)* until day three

Applies to Jewish people in the land of Israel at a time when the Sanhedrin holds civil jurisdiction.

- N23 – Deuteronomy 13:16 – Not rebuilding an apostate or idolatrous city
- P186 – Deuteronomy 13:16 – Not following the law of the apostate city
- N24 – Deuteronomy 13:17 – Not deriving benefit from the property of an apostate city

Applies to Jewish people in the land of Israel with the temple and Levitical system in place.

- P83 – Deuteronomy 12:5–6 – Bringing due offerings on the first festival to Jerusalem without delay
- N229 – Deuteronomy 12:19 – Not forsaking or leaving the Levites without their due support

Applies to Jews and God-fearing Gentiles in the Diaspora with the temple and Levitical system in place.

- P85 – Deuteronomy 12:26 – Bringing a required offering from outside the land to the temple

Applies to Jewish people in the land of Israel.

- P185 – Deuteronomy 12:3 – Destroying all idols and their places of worship

CHAPTER 6

Judges

"Shoftim"
Deuteronomy 16:18–21:9

Many new commandments are given in this parsha addressing fundamental issues concerning leadership for the Israelites. Parsha Shoftim begins with the law to appoint judges (*shoftim*) and officers once they enter the Promised Land. Moses instructs the people to pursue justice. These judges were to be appointed based upon cities according to the tribes. The parsha quickly moves onto the prohibition of idolatrous forms of worship, sorcery, and the law against offering blemished animals. Shoftim also covers the appointment of the kings and their responsibilities. There are instructions about how many horses and wives the king should take. Also found is the charge for the king to write out his own copies of Torah. There is discussion about the priestly gifts, the prophet like Moses, cities of refuge, boundaries, issues concerning warfare, unsolved crimes, and the prohibition of cutting down the fruit tree when laying siege.

I cannot go into detail for all the commandments given in Shoftim due to the limits of this book, so discussion will be limited to the judicial system and the prophets, giving time and attention to developing an understanding of the concept of *teshuva* and the month of Elul.

Judicial System

In this parsha, the Torah gives the formal command to establish the courts and appoint the Sanhedrin, or high court, for each tribe. Shoftim develops the judge (judicial and legislative), the king (executive), the priest (ritual), and the prophet (religious) as forms of leadership for the Jewish people. In addition to the Sanhedrin, officers would be appointed to enforce the decisions that were made. Sforno understood the power of these leaders as the reason the majority of this sidra deals with the commandments directed at these leaders.[147] In the Chumash, Rambam stressed the need for the people to obey the Sanhedrin. He stated that the power to interpret the Torah was given to the sages, and if some people decided not to follow their rules, all of society would break down and anarchy would reign. We can read about this very thing happening at the end of the book of Judges, when there was no king and everyone did what was right in his or her own eyes (Judges 21:25). These judges were to ensure that Israel would become a holy nation set apart to bring honor to God. The Mishnah claims the world endures by virtue of three things: law, truth, and peace.[148]

The sages taught that appointing a judge who was not Torah observant is synonymous with planting an idolatrous tree.[149] This would mean the death penalty for the idol worshiper and for the man who appoints the unrighteous judge because it denies the existence of God. The Chumash claims that the forceful language implies that no obligation or threat can ever justify idolatry.[150] Shoftim then covers the qualifications for the king. He must be an Israelite and he cannot acquire many horses or wives lest his heart turn away from the Lord.

The most important qualification would be that he must continue to study Torah. He must write for himself two handwritten scrolls, one of which is to be kept with him at all times to read from every day, all the days of his life, so he will learn to fear the Lord and to keep the words of the Torah (18–19). Deuteronomy 27:26 would no doubt remind them of the consequences if they did not keep the words of the Torah. Here the

---

[147] Scherman, Sforno. *Chumash*, 2000, 1024.

[148] Mishnah. *Ethics of the Fathers.* Pirkei Avot 1:18. http://www.chabad.org/library/article_cdo/aid/2165/jewish/Chapter-One.htm (accessed May 29, 2014).

[149] A. Cohen and A. Mishcon. *Soncino Babylonian Talmud Abodah Zarah.* Kindle ed. Teaneck, New Jersey: Talmudic Books, 2012, 52a20. Kindle location 9283.

[150] Scherman. *Chumash*, 2000, 1025.

text refers to the entire Torah in terms of its contents.[151] It is obvious by Paul's writing that he thought the law (Torah) encompassed more than the first five books of Moses as he quoted Isaiah 28:11 in 1 Corinthians 14:21 referring to it as law. "In the Law it is written, 'By men of strange tongues and by the lips of strangers I will speak to this people ... '" Then in 2 Timothy 3:16, he reminds the reader that all Scripture is inspired and profitable for teaching, for reproof, for correction, and for training in righteousness.

In Moses' day, if one wanted unlimited access to the Word of God, they would have to write it out themselves. Today, there is no excuse for not having at least one copy of the entire counsel of God. The commandment for the king to write out his own copy of the Torah demonstrates the work of Jesus, who is the Word made flesh, writing a copy of the Torah on every believer's heart. As Jesus lives inside the believer, the believer's body is the sanctuary where the consecration emphasis should be placed. Perhaps that process should start as all believers write out a copy of Torah to carry with them and study all the days of their lives.

After discussion of the judge, the king, and the priest, *Shoftim* moves on to discuss the manner in which God will communicate His will in the future. Knowing that people inherently want to know what the future holds, it seems plausible that they would consult the sorcerers, diviners, and witches. God makes it clear that He will send a prophet like Moses. The text explains that the prophet will come from among their own people (Deuteronomy 18:15), implying that the life and ministry of Moses is a foreshadowing or prototype of the Messiah.

The New Testament reiterates the need for the leaders as well as the need for those laypeople to be submissive to their authority (Romans 13:1). In 1 Timothy 2, Paul urges the people to be in prayer for those in leadership so they may live in peace.

---

[151] Jacob Chinitz. The Word Torah in the Torah. Jewish Bible Quarterly, Vol. 33, No 4, 2005. 244.

Elul and Teshuva

This parsha comes at the beginning of the month of Elul. Elul is a month of repentance (*teshuva*) that precedes the Jewish high holidays of Rosh Hashanah (the Feast of Trumpets) and Yom Kippur (the Day of Atonement). Jewish tradition tells us that Elul represents the time that Moses spent on Mount Sinai receiving the second set of tablets containing the Law of God. It is believed that Moses ascended the mountain for a third time forty days after the sin of the golden calf on 1 Elul. After forty days, he returned on 10 Tishri, Yom Kippur, with the second set of tablets. Therefore, the month of Elul still represents a national month of *teshuva* and soul searching, or *cheshbon hanafesh*. This is a time to offer prayers for forgiveness *(selichot* or *slixot* prayers). Beginning on 1 Elul, it is customary to blow the shofar (ram's horn) every day, all month long, with the exception of the Sabbath. According to Rambam, the shofar blowing was done as a wake-up call for teshuva, selichot, and charity. It is customary to read the Psalms during this season of repentance. The Hebrew word *slichah* means "excuse me" in conversational Hebrew, but in Psalm 130:4, it refers specifically to God's grace for the repentant sinner. "But with you there is forgiveness, that you may be feared." The word *selichot* then refers specifically to additional prayer recited during the month of Elul.

The selichot prayers help the worshipers focus their minds on repentance for themselves and for the people of Israel. This is when followers examine their behavior in the last year and seek forgiveness from God, at the same time promising to improve their behavior in the next year. The sages say that the way you meet the first day of the New Year (Rosh Hashanah) sets the tone for the entire year; if you are joyful and at peace on Rosh Hashanah, the rest of the year will be peaceful and joyful as well. According to the Talmud, the list of the Thirteen Attributes of God's Mercy, known as *Shelosh Esrei Middot shel Rachamim*, is the primary focus of the selichot prayer.[152] Talmud states, "Whenever the nation of Israel sins let them pray *Shelosh Esrei Middot shel Rachamim* and I shall forgive them." Thus, today the Selichot Service is built around Scripture of Exodus 34:6–7.

---

[152] Maurice Simon. *Soncino Babylonian Talmud: Rosh Hashanah,* 17b, Kindle ed. Teaneck, New Jersey: Talmudic Books, 2012. Kindle location 2053.

> Then the LORD passed by in front of him and proclaimed, "The LORD, the LORD God, compassionate and gracious, slow to anger, and abounding in loving-kindness and truth; who keeps lovingkindness for thousands, who forgives iniquity, transgression and sin; yet He will by no means leave the guilty unpunished, visiting the iniquity of fathers on the children and on the grandchildren to the third and fourth generations.

In addition to the selichot prayers, reading Psalm 130 and other poems is customary.

> Out of the depths I have cried to You, O LORD. LORD, hear my voice! Let Your ears be attentive to the voice of my supplications. If You, LORD, should mark iniquities, O LORD, who could stand? But there is forgiveness with You, that You may be feared. I wait for the LORD, my soul does wait, and in His word do I hope. My soul *waits* for the LORD more than the watchmen for the morning; indeed, more than the watchmen for the morning. O Israel, hope in the LORD; for with the LORD there is loving-kindness, and with Him is abundant redemption. And He will redeem Israel from all his iniquities.

Repentance

Repentance is foundational for the Jew. R. Adda b. Ahaba compared the unrepentant sinner to a man holding a dead reptile. He claimed that this man could not be cleaned even if he immersed himself in all the waters of the world, yet if he would throw away the snake, he could become clean once immersed. Ahaba said, "Whosoever confesseth and forsaketh them shall obtain mercy."[153]

The overall theme of Deuteronomy is teshuva—a calling to return to

---

[153] Joseph Rabbinowitz. *Soncino Babylonian Talmud Taanith,* Kindle ed. Teaneck, New Jersey: Talmudic Books, 2012. Kindle location 2032.

God after a period of falling away or just a lack of commitment. Essentially, sin is failure. Teshuva has four distinct aspects: regret and acknowledging that a mistake was made; cessation or stopping the harmful or sinful action as a way to display commitment to change; confession or admitting mistakes verbally; and finally, resolution to be deliberate and committed not to repeat the same mistake or harmful action again.

The Hebrew word *chet*, translated as "sin," literally means "failure in relationship with the Lord." As *chet* causes one to fail or move away from the Lord, teshuva means "to return." Often translated as repentance, it is more accurately understood as turning back (*shuv*) to God. Over one thousand times we see the root of this word in Scripture. Regarded as a turning away from evil and turning toward good, Jewish thought regards turning to God as the means by which one turns away from evil.[154]

The Greek word *metanoia*, translated as "repentance," literally means "changing your thinking." Metanoia is often the Greek word used to translate the Hebrew word *nacham* and is often associated with the emotion of regret. In some translations, nacham is translated to the word "repent" rather than "changing one's mind." The Greek verb *strepho* often expresses the Hebrew idea of *shuv* (turning to God and away from evil). Essentially, *nacham* in Hebrew, or *metanoia* in the Greek, concerns the past (regret), whereas *shuv* in the Hebrew, or *strepho* in the Greek, concerns the present.[155]

The parsha Shoftim emphasizes the necessity to empower and submit to authority. According to Torah and the New Testament, the first authority we are to submit to is our own intellect, our mind, and our thoughts (2 Corinthians 10:5). The mind by nature rules the heart; taking captive our thoughts empowers and frees the believer to steer his or her life in the way of the Lord. This is not a submission to totalitarian oppression; rather, it is a submission to become all that God intended each individual to be. Intrinsically, our souls desire God and to do His will, yet our nature is to sin, so true freedom can only be found in an ongoing state of teshuva—a cycle that is never finished. Paul cried out, "I am not practicing what I

---

[154] John Parsons. *Elul and Selichot: The Season of Teshuvah*—Hebrew for Christians. http://www.hebrew4christians.com/Holidays/Fall_Holidays/Elul/Elul.pdf, 10.
[155] Ibid.

would like to do, but I am doing the very thing I hate" (Romans 7:15). Paul understood the power of the flesh and the bondage of sin. In Romans chapter 7, he was in a state of teshuva. Teshuva is a type of rebirth—a death of the past life and the birth of the new (2 Corinthians 5:17). Teshuva is the power of the Holy Spirit working through the heart of the believer: perpetual and timeless, as we will never get beyond the call to repent and believe the gospel (Mark 1:15) this side of heaven.[156]

A Prophet Like Moses

Deuteronomy 18:15–19 explains that God will "raise up a prophet like Moses" that the children of Israel were to obey. Jesus resembled Moses in many ways. Looking into the similarities, we can find that both were Jews (Exodus 2:2; Hebrews 11:23; Matthew 2:13–14), prophets (Deuteronomy 34:10; Matthew 21:11), and priests (Hebrews 4:14). Both were leaders, lawgivers, and mediators between God and man (Exodus 24:7–8; Matthew 26:26–28; Mark 14:24; Luke 22:20). Like Moses, Jesus was sent from God to speak His words (Exodus 3:1–10; John 8:42) and teach the people (Deuteronomy 4:1–5; John 3:2; Matthew 22:16). Both men were born under foreign rule (Exodus 1:8–14; Luke 2:1), spent their childhood in Egypt (Exodus 2:10; Matthew 2:14–15), and were threatened by evil kings (Exodus 1:15–16; Matthew 2:16). Initially, both men were rejected by their families (Numbers 12:1; Mark 3:20–21). The Jewish population rejected them (Exodus 31:1; Matthew 27:21–22), yet the Gentiles accepted them (Exodus 2:14–22; Acts 10:45). Moses and Jesus were humble servants of the God (Numbers 12:3; Luke 2:46–47) and shepherds of Israel (Exodus 3:1; Numbers; John 10:10–11; Matthew 9:36). Both men were sent from a mountain of God to free Israel—Moses from Mount Sinai and Jesus from Mount Zion. They were faithful to God (Numbers 12:5–7; Hebrews 3:1–2) and revealed His name (Exodus 3:13–14; John 17:6. 11–12) as they gave bread from heaven (Exodus 16:14–15; Matthew 14:19–20) and worked many miracles (Exodus 4:21–8; Deuteronomy 34:10–12; John 5:36; 12:37–38). Both fasted for forty days in the wilderness (Exodus 34:28; Matthew 4:2) and were appointed as saviors of Israel. Both men

---

[156] Parsons. *Elul and Selichot,* 2014, 12.

knew God face-to-face (Exodus 3:1–10; Luke 9:34–36). Moses saved the people from the bondage to Egypt; Jesus saved them from their bondage to sin. Moses sent twelve spies to Canaan (Numbers 13); Jesus sent twelve apostles to the world (Matthew 10:1). Moses appointed seventy rulers over Israel (Numbers 11:16–17), and Jesus sent seventy disciples to the ends of the earth (Luke 10:1). Moses instituted Passover as a means by which the angel of death would pass over the homes of those who believed in the shed blood of the lamb (Exodus 12:11–12). Jesus offered himself as the lamb who would redeem them permanently and save them from their sin (John 1:29). Just as Moses brought the Torah to Israel fifty days after the Exodus from Egypt (known as Shavu'ot), Jesus sent the Holy Spirit fifty days after His resurrection (known as Pentecost). Both Moses and Jesus offered to die for the people's sin (Exodus 32:30–33; John 17). To say that these similarities are amazing is an understatement.

Mitzvot[157]

Applies to everyone in every time and place.

- P173 – Deuteronomy 17:15 – Appointing a king
- N246 – Deuteronomy 19:14 – Not moving a neighbor's landmark

Applies to both Jews and Gentiles in every place and time.

- N32 – Deuteronomy 18:10 – Not practicing clairvoyance
- N33 – Deuteronomy 18:10 – Not practicing magic
- N34 – Deuteronomy 18:10 – Not practicing spell casting
- N35 – Deuteronomy 18:10 – Not practicing the art of a charmer
- N37 – Deuteronomy 18:10 – Not consulting wizards
- N38 – Deuteronomy 18:10 – Not consulting the dead
- N36 – Deuteronomy 18:10 – Not consulting mediums or necromancers
- P176 – Deuteronomy 16:18 – To appoint judges

---

[157] Numbered by Rambam. Grouped by applicability according to First Fruits of Zion.

- N26 – Deuteronomy 18:20 – Not prophesying in the names of idols
- N27 – Deuteronomy 18:20 – Not prophesying falsely in the name of the Lord
- N29 – Deuteronomy 18:22 – Not fearing putting a false prophet to death

Applies to both Jewish and God-fearing Gentile judges in every time and place.

- N288 – Deuteronomy 19:15 – Not passing judgment on the word of one witness
- N11 – Deuteronomy 16:22 – Not erecting a standing stone for people to revere
- P174 – Deuteronomy 17:10–11 – Obeying the Great Sanhedrin
- N312 – Deuteronomy 17:11 – Not disobeying the Great Sanhedrin
- P171 – Deuteronomy 18:15 – Heeding the true prophets

Applies to Jewish people in every place and time.

- N362 – Deuteronomy 17:15 – Not appointing a non-Israelite as a king over Israel
- N46 – Deuteronomy 17:16 – Not dwelling in Egypt
- N57 – Deuteronomy 20:19 – Not destroying fruit trees even in times of war

Applies to the king of Israel in every place and time.

- N363 – Deuteronomy 17:16 – Not having too many horses
- N364 – Deuteronomy 17:17 – The king of Israel may not multiply wives to himself
- N365 – Deuteronomy 17:17 – The king of Israel may not amass undue wealth to himself
- P17 – Deuteronomy 17:18 – Writing a personal copy of the scroll of the Torah

Applies to the priesthood in Jerusalem with the temple and Levitical system in place.

- N95 – Deuteronomy 17:1 – Not sacrificing an animal with a temporary blemish
- P36 – Deuteronomy 18:6–8 – Serving according to divisions

Applies to Jewish livestock owners with five or more sheep in the land of Israel.

- P144 – Deuteronomy 18:4 – Giving the first of every sheering to the priesthood

Applies to Jewish people in the land of Israel.

- P182 – Deuteronomy 19:3 – Establishing the six cities of refuge

Applies to Jews and God-fearing Gentile believers in Jerusalem.

- N13 – Deuteronomy 16:21 – Not planting a tree in the temple courtyard

Applies to Jews and God-fearing Gentile believers in the land of Israel.

- N309 – Deuteronomy 21:4 – Not plowing the place where the heifer was killed

Applies to Jewish farmers doing agriculture in the land of Israel, and by rabbinic extension, in Babylon and territories annexed by King David.

- P126 – Deuteronomy 18:4 – Separating the great *terumah* for the priesthood

Applies to the army of Israel at a time when the Jewish people occupy the land.

- P190 – Deuteronomy 20:11 – Waging war according to the law of the Torah
- N49 – Deuteronomy 20:16 – Not sparing the lives of any of the seven Canaanite nations

Applies to the elders and judges of a Jewish city in the land of Israel when Jewish people live in the land.

- P181 – Deuteronomy 21:4 – Decapitating a calf for an unsolved murder

Applies to the Jewish people in the land of Israel with the temple and Levitical system in place.

- N169 – Deuteronomy 18:1 – Not allotting the Levites an inheritance of land

Applies to the priesthood at a time when the Jewish people occupy the land.

- P191 – Deuteronomy 20:2–4 – Anointing a priest for war

Applies to the Jewish people in the land of Israel with the temple and Levitical system in place.

- N110 – Deuteronomy 18:1 – Not allotting the Levites a share in the spoils of war

Applies to Jewish butchers in the land of Israel.

- P143 – Deuteronomy 18:3 – Giving the priests certain portions from every ritually slaughtered animal

Applies to both Jewish and Gentile judges in a court of law when the murderer has been convicted by due process.

- N279 – Deuteronomy 19:13 – Having no pity on a murderer

CHAPTER 7

When You Go

"Ki Tetze"
Deuteronomy 21:10–25:19

In Hebrew, Ki Tetze means "when you go." This parsha contains more commandments than any other parsha. It can seem overwhelming to think that there would be any way one could keep all these commandments. However, a theme of mercy is interwoven throughout this parsha that cannot be ignored. There are no fewer than seventy-four commandments in Ki Tetze. These include the laws of the captive women, the rights of the firstborn, the rebellious son, capital punishment, and the concern for property. Laws on sexual purity, cross-dressing, marriage and divorce, and the sanctity of the camp are also included in this parsha. Commandments concerning fair wages, individual responsibility, and the idea of being "unequally yoked" are found in Ki Tetze. The instruction to wear the tzitzit, the concept of *lashon hara*, and the obligation to always remember are found in this parsha as well. There are so many laws in this parsha that one could perhaps write a series of books on any of them, so I will focus this section on three of these principles: the mercy of God, lashon hara, and the mandate to remember.

Mercy

The parsha starts out with a response to the evil inclination of a soldier[158] when he sees a woman among the enemies and feels that he has desire for her. The Chumash claims this law is designed to make the soldier wait before he is intimate with her so his desire will diminish and he will set her free.[159] Still other commentators say it is merely a rite of passage, marking the woman's transformation from an alien woman to the wife of an Israelite.[160] The wait is a month long, and the woman is to mourn the loss of her parents, shave her head, and grow her nails. If in her month of slovenly appearance, the soldier becomes disinterested in her, he has no right to keep her imprisoned; he is to set her free. If he is still attracted to her, he can marry her, provided she is willing to convert and obey the Torah.[161]

God's mercy can be seen as he sets the laws for the firstborn son. The firstborn is to receive a double portion (Deuteronomy 21:17). The Chumash states that God supports the brokenhearted by commanding that the double portion go to the firstborn son, even if the firstborn son is not born to a favored wife. Even in the case of the rebellious son, there is much to learn and mercy to find. The sages say there are two teachings on this. One says that the execution is not because of the child's grievous sin but because his behavior makes it clear that he will degenerate into a monstrous human being.[162] The second teaching says that there are so many detailed requirements in this passage that it is virtually impossible for such a case to occur.[163] Rabbi Bachya cites a "tough love" for parents as their love for God must supersede their love of child. They must always be willing to turn the child over to the court,[164] as Abraham did Isaac.

---

158 Scherman, Sifre. *Chumash*, 2000, 1046.

159 Scherman. *Chumash*, 2000, 1046.

160 Robert Alter. *The Five Books of Moses: A Translation with Commentary*. New York: W. W. Norton & Company, 2008, 982.

161 Scherman, Rambam. *Chumash*, 2000, 1047.

162 Jacob Shachter and H. Freedman. *Soncino Babylonian Talmud Sanhedrin* 72a, Kindle ed. Talmudic Books, 2012. Kindle location 19358.

163 Ibid. Kindle location 19105.

164 Scherman, R' Bachya. *Chumash*, 2000, 1048.

God's mercy can surely be seen in the directive to build a safety fence around the roofs of homes lest anyone fall. They did not have pitched roofs as we see in our contemporary homes; rather, the roofs were flat and very much a part of their living space. The Torah places the responsibility for the safety of the guest on the homeowner. This calls for the elimination of carelessness. Be mindful of things that might hurt others, then fix the broken, and protect all who pass by. This law also argues against the deterministic viewpoint. Leibowitz argues that if it was predetermined that a man should fall from a roof, why have a law that demands one build the fence in the first place?[165]

In an attempt to avoid promiscuity and to preserve the normal differences between man and woman, the Torah forbids the man to wear a woman's garment or women to wear men's garb. The sages will apply this to men who are excessively interested in personal grooming and to women who wear battle dress.[166]

In Ki Tetze, it is commanded not to yoke together an ox and a donkey. The idea is that the farmer could use either animal, but yoking them together would result in crooked furrows and injured animals. We can see this concept brought out in the idea to take on the yoke of the Torah, and from the New Testament not to be yoked together with unbelievers (2 Corinthians 6:14–15). Where being yoked to the Torah could bring a straight path and righteous living, being yoked with an unbeliever would result in heartache and disunity, whether yoked in marriage, business, cultural practices, diet, rituals, or worship. This parsha discusses marriage and divorce and remarriage laws. Specifically, this law was intended to prevent people from marrying just to "test-drive" a new partner only to discard the partner if it does not work out the way they had hoped. These laws (P222-Deuteronomy 24:1, N356-Deuteronomy 24:4) apply to everyone in every place and every time, although one could never tell by looking at our culture today. God forbade intermarriage with the Moabite (male), but God's mercy can still be seen in the forgiveness of the Moabitess (female),

---

[165] Yeshayahu Leibowitz. *Accepting the Yoke of Heaven*. Jerusalem: Urim Publications, 2006, 181.

[166] Klien, B. D. *Soncino Babylonian: Talmud Nazir* 59a, Kindle ed. Teaneck, New Jersey: Talmudic Books, 2012. Kindle location 8136.

who would not have been involved in the killing of the weak, the women, and the children.

God's mercy is seen in the text of individual responsibility. Yes, the concept of arevut discussed in parasha Re'eh is still true, but here we see that ultimate responsibility lies with the individual sinner. Each person has free will to make choices and will be held accountable for his or her own actions. The concept of arevut applies in the commanded concern for widows, orphans (24:17–18), and the poor (19–22) and even in the punishment of the guilty (25:1–3) and working animals (4).

Evil Speech

The concept of lashon hara has to do with defamation of character, or literally "bad talk." In our culture, we call it gossip. Slander or evil speech (lashon hara) is forbidden in the Torah, even if the slanderous remarks are true. It is forbidden to repeat anything about another, even if it is not bad. This is called talebearing. Talebearing in Hebrew is *rakhil*, which is related to a word meaning "trader." Listening to lashon hara is equally bad. One should either rebuke the speaker or refuse to listen.[167] Proverbs 6:12–15 indicates it is lashon hara to make a derogatory motion to or about someone. This might even include the infamous eye-roll in response to someone's inappropriate behavior or response. A main argument is that lashon hara begins with envy; therefore, giving the dreaded "evil eye" is also considered lashon hara.[168] Philo writes that it is not language that provokes such evil but the emulation and rivalry of souls in wrongdoing. He adds that even those who have had their tongues cut out can still do as much damage with their body language.[169] There are only a few exceptions to this commandment, such as in the case of a testimony in a court of law. The laws of lashon hara are lengthy, and many commentaries are published each year on this topic alone.

---

[167] Rabbi Yisrael Meir Kagan and Rabbi Shraga Silerstein. *Chafetz Chaim*, Kindle ed. Jerusalem: Silverstein, 2014. Kindle location 136.

[168] Bruce J. Malina. *The New Testament World: Insights from Cultural Anthropology.* Louisville: Westminster John Knox Press. 2001, 118.

[169] C. D. Yonge. *The Works of Philo: On the Confusion of Tongues,* Kindle ed. Peabody: Hendrickson Publishers, 2013. Kindle location 10102.

In this parsha, verses 13–29 speak to the severe punishment for making up a story about someone (lashon hara) to escape one's responsibility. The sin of lashon hara has been the subject not only of many commentaries but also of many tragedies in Israel and around the world. The spies that accompanied Joshua and Caleb spoke lashon hara about the Promised Land, which provoked the whole camp to grumble (lashon hara), thereby sealing their fate in the wilderness. Other historical events cited as lashon hara include Joseph's negative reports (also known as tattling or lashon hara) about his brothers, which caused them to hate him and eventually sell him as a slave. According to the Talmud, it was slander of the Jews by the Jews that brought about the destruction of the second temple.[170] More recent was the Six Day War in June of 1967, a tragedy that began with lashon hara. The Chumash states that death and life are in the power of the tongue.[171]

The laws regarding proper speech are by far the hardest laws of Torah to keep. On Yom Kippur, all Jews recite the Al Cheit confession. There are forty-three sins itemized in this confession. Of the forty-three, eleven are sins committed through speech. The Talmud states that the tongue is so dangerous that it must be hidden out of view and behind a set of teeth (Psalm 39:1). Speech is often compared to an arrow (Psalms 64:3); once released, there is no drawing it back, and words, like arrows often go astray. The tongue is compared to a sword (Psalm 7:4), like a sharpened razor (Psalm 52:2), and the pen of a skillful writer (Psalm 45:1). It is as sharp as the serpent's poisonous bite (Psalm 140:3), full of deadly poison, and impossible to tame (James 3:8). The tongue is a fire capable of defiling the entire body and sets on fire the course of our lives (James 3:6). Coarse jesting (Ephesians 5:4) would include calling a person a derogatory nickname. Torah forbids it even when everyone else uses the same nickname. Coarse jesting is forbidden even when one is just being silly. To embarrass someone, even in an attempt to defend another, is sin. The law forbids one to provoke his or her children (Ephesians 6:4). To deceive a person, even when no harm is done, would be considered lashon hara (e.g., sending

---

[170] Maurice Simon. *Soncino Babylonian Talmud Gittin* 55b–56a, Kindle ed. Teaneck: Talmudic Books, 2012. Kindle location 8535.

[171] Scherman. *Chumash*, 2000, 1060.

someone on a snipe hunt). Even to compliment a person when you do not really mean it would be a sin. More than 140 times the Scripture refers to the use of the tongue. The Talmud declares that lashon hara kills three: the person who speaks it, the person who listens, and the person about whom it is said.[172] When Miriam doubted and spoke "evil" and discouraging words to her brother Moses, God rebuked her. Her punishment was leprosy (*tzaraat*) (24:8). Because of the intercessory prayer of her brother, God healed her, but she still had to spend seven days outside the camp. Colossians 4:6 insists that speech be made with grace and seasoned with salt. While this may be impossible to master according to James (3:2), we are to do our best and then forgive others when they to fall short.

The Torah is clear when it says, "Remember what God, your God, did to Miriam on the way, when you were leaving Egypt." Jews and Christians alike are to remember it all.

Matthew 12:36 addresses the concept of lashon hara as Matthew reminds the reader that everyone will be accountable for every careless word spoken. Ryrie argues that some sins are more sinful than others, citing Jesus' teaching in Matthew 7:1–5 on the speck and the log as well as John 19:11, calling Caiaphas's sin of delivering Jesus to the authorities as greater than Pilate's. Ryrie also cites sins of speech as examples of greater sins (Matthew 12:22–37).[173]

Today, it seems people tend to focus on the less desirable qualities in others. In politics, the candidates run their campaigns based not on what they can do for the people but on what their opponent has not done. Slander has become a method to make money and earn ratings. Reality TV and lashon hara go hand in hand. A popular cooking show builds on the verbal bashing of fellow cooks. Unfortunately, the church and the pulpit are not exempt from lashon hara. A preacher on the pulpit once referred to a less demonstrative congregation as "the church of the Frozen Chosen." He was only teasing, but it was still lashon hara and sin.

Lashon hara happens in families and in marriage. A family member or

---

[172] Leo Jung, Maurice Simon, and L. Miller. *Soncino Babylonian Talmud Bekoroth and Arakin* 15b, Kindle ed. Teaneck: Talmudic Books, 2012. Kindle location 13578.
[173] Charles C. Ryrie. *Basic Theology: A Popular Systematic Guide to Understanding Biblical Truth,* Kindle ed. Chicago: Moody Publishers, 1999. Kindle location 4026.

spouse can do most things right, yet it seems that the minute one makes a mistake or does something considered stupid, the family unity can dissolve. I have seen families hold hostage the words of another while years go by without meaningful communication. Even the absence of words is lashon hara as others observe the deliberate silence.

Remember

Remembering is another prevalent theme in the Scriptures. Over two hundred times the Scriptures tell us to remember. In this parsha, Moses reminded them to wear their *tzitzit* (the tassel that hangs from the four corners of the *tallit*, or prayer shawl) throughout their generations. It is ordered to look at the tzitzit and remember all the commandments of the Lord, to obey them and not to follow their deceitful heart and eyes, that all might be holy to God (Numbers 15:38–40). It is vital to take captive every thought (2 Corinthians 10:5) and cultivate thoughts to remember the rest God gives, his marvelous works, and especially the trials we endure, lest everyone forget and turn back to doing what is right in his own eyes (Judges 21:25). God is a visual God and knows the human propensity to wander. Therefore, He has given many props, like the tzitzit, to remind one to be deliberate about behavior and thoughts, speaking and acting as those who are going to be judged by the law that gives freedom (James 2:12–13).

The parsha Ki Titze concludes with the command to remember Amalek and his deeds. Amalek was the vilest of all Israel's enemies. The fact that Amalek attacked the weak, faint, and weary stragglers was most offensive to God (25:17). Thus the command "You must not forget" (19). If Amalek feared God instead of people and fought fair with a full frontal assault, it would have gone better for him.[174] There is much to learn from this battle and then applied to the life of the Christian. Spiritual warfare is like the Amalekites, always looking for the opportunity to sneak up from the rear and attack when one is weary. One can see that this battle was fought in the light. As long as Moses had his hands in the air praising God, the Israelites prevailed. When Moses got weary, the Amalekites gained ground, so in those weary moments, Aaron and Hur held his

---

[174] Scherman, R' Yitzchak Zev Soloveitchik. *Chumash*, 2000, 1067.

arms up for him. In the same way, Christians should never stop meeting together and praying for each other, so when one does grow weary, others will help the Christian be steadfast in faith. The Scriptures command one to remember what this means. To fulfill this commandment on Shabbat Zachor, the Shabbat before Purim (the festival remembering how Esther saved the people), it is Jewish tradition to read the Scripture from Exodus 20:8, remember the Shabbat and keep it holy; Exodus 13:3, remember the Passover; Deuteronomy 24:9, remember what God did to Miriam; and Deuteronomy 25:17, remember what Amalek did to Israel. Thus, the Jewish tradition of celebrating Purim is a time for wiping out the memory of Haman the Agagite (Esther 3:1), a descendant of Amalek, and the memory of Amalek himself. For the Christian, the battle is not with the rulers of this world but with the forces of darkness, and our weapon is the truth of salvation in Christ Jesus.

The Haftarah reading for Ki Tetze (Isaiah 54:10) is a beautiful reminder of God's mercy. Jerusalem is compared to a woman without a child and a widow who lost her husband as God commands her to rejoice. The prophet Isaiah tells the woman she will not remember the shame of her youth. The people are reminded of the covenant God has made with them. As the Lord made a promise with Noah, so did he make a promise to the children of Israel. The Israelites will be regathered and restored in the end of days, and all of Israel will be saved. This is a beautiful message during the month of Elul as the Jewish people repent and search for God's freedom.

Mitzvot[175]

Applies to everyone in every time and place.

- P231 – Deuteronomy 21:23 – Arranging proper burial for a corpse
- P204 – Deuteronomy 22:1 – Returning lost property to its owner
- N269 – Deuteronomy 22:3 – Not ignoring lost property

---

[175] Numbered by Rambam. Grouped by applicability according to First Fruits of Zion.

Applies to men in every place and time.

- P213 – Deuteronomy 22:13 – Marrying a woman
- N40 – Deuteronomy 22:5 – Not putting on a woman's garments

Applies to women in every time and place.

- N39 – Deuteronomy 22:5 – Not putting on a man's garments

Applies to Jewish women in every time and place.

- N53 – Deuteronomy 23:3 – Not marrying a male Ammonite or Moabite, even if he becomes a proselyte

Applies to both Jews and God-fearing Gentiles in Jerusalem in every time.

- N78 – Deuteronomy 23:10 – Not entering the camp of the Levites while ritually unclean

Applies to both Jews and God-fearing Gentiles in every time and place.

- N356 – Deuteronomy 24:4 – Not remarrying one's divorced wife after she has remarried
- N219 – Deuteronomy 25:4 – Not preventing a beast from eating from the produce in which it is working
- N270 – Deuteronomy 22:4 – Not leaving the beast of your neighbor lying under its burden
- P203 – Deuteronomy 22:4 – Helping your neighbor load his beast
- N306 – Deuteronomy 22:6 – Not taking a mother bird with her young
- P148 – Deuteronomy 22:7 – Sending the mother bird away
- N218 – Deuteronomy 22:10 – Not yoking two kinds of animals together
- P94 – Deuteronomy 23:23 – Fulfilling one's words
- P198 – Deuteronomy 23:20 – Charging interest only to foreigners
- N255 – Deuteronomy 23:16 – Not oppressing a fugitive slave

- N355 – Deuteronomy 23:17 – Not having sexual relations outside of marriage
- N236 – Deuteronomy 23:19 – Not borrowing from a brother at interest
- P222 – Deuteronomy 24:1 – Writing a certificate of divorce
- P247 – Deuteronomy 25:12 – Saving the life of one who is pursued by a killer, even if the killer needs to be killed
- N293 – Deuteronomy 25:12 – Not sparing the life of a pursuing killer
- N272 – Deuteronomy 25:13 – Not owning inaccurate weights or measures

Applies to both Jews and Gentiles in every time and place.

- N294 – Deuteronomy 22:26 – Not punishing someone who was forced to commit a transgression

Applies to both Jewish and God-fearing Gentile believers serving as hired workers.

- N267 – Deuteronomy 23:25 – Not eating of the produce while working
- N268 – Deuteronomy 23:24 – Not taking more produce than one can eat at once

Applies to property-owners in every place and time.

- P184 – Deuteronomy 22:8 – Building a guardrail around a roof
- N298 – Deuteronomy 22:8 – Not leaving a stumbling block

Applies to both Jewish and God-fearing Gentile lenders in every time and place.

- N242 – Deuteronomy 24:6 – Not taking items needed for food preparation as a pledge
- N241 – Deuteronomy 24:17 – Not taking a widow's pledge

- N239 – Deuteronomy 24:10 – Not taking a pledge by force
- N240 – Deuteronomy 24:12 – Not withholding a borrower's pledge when the man needs it
- P199 – Deuteronomy 24:13 – Returning a pledge to its owner when he needs it

Applies to Jews and God-fearing Gentile believers in a time and place where Torah courts hold the civil authority to enforce them.

- P218 – Deuteronomy 22:29 – The seducer of an unbetrothed virgin must pay the fine and marry her
- N358 – Deuteronomy 22:29 – The seducer of an unbetrothed girl cannot send her away

Applies to Jewish people in every time and place.

- N42 – Deuteronomy 22:11 – Not wearing wool and linen woven together
- N354 – Deuteronomy 23:2 – A mamzer may not marry a Jew
- P189 – Deuteronomy 25:17 – Remembering what Amalek did to the Israelites when they went forth from Egypt
- P188 – Deuteronomy 25:19 – On the extinction of Amalek's seed
- N59 – Deuteronomy 25:19 – Not forgetting what Amalek did to the Israelites when they went forth from Egypt
- N55 – Deuteronomy 23:7 – Not excluding Egyptians and refusing to intermarry with them beyond two generations
- N56 – Deuteronomy 23:6 – Not making peace treaties with Ammon or Moab
- N54 – Deuteronomy 23:7–8 – Not excluding Edomites and refusing to intermarry with them beyond two generations
- P216 – Deuteronomy 25:5 – To observe the Levirate marriage

Applies specifically to the judges on the Sanhedrin, but the broader principle of according dignity to the dead applies universally.

- N66 – Deuteronomy 21:23 – Not leaving a corpse hanging overnight

Applies to both Jewish husbands and believing Gentile husbands in the land of Israel when the Jewish people occupy the land.

- P214 – Deuteronomy 24:5 – Rejoicing with his wife for the first year of marriage

Applies to Jewish and Gentile soldiers in the army of the Lord during temple times.

- P192 – Deuteronomy 23:12 – Preparing a latrine outside the camp
- P193 – Deuteronomy 23:13 – Keeping a digging tool among the weapons

Applies to Jewish people in the land of Israel and by rabbinic extension in every land.

- N216 – Deuteronomy 22:9 – Not sowing grain or vegetables in a vineyard
- N193 – Deuteronomy 22:9 – Not eating produce from grain or vegetables sown in a vineyard

Applies to Jewish and Gentile judges in a court of law in every time and place.

- N280 – Deuteronomy 24:17 – Not perverting the justice due to strangers and orphans

Applies to Jewish and God-fearing Gentile employers in every time and place.

- P200 – Deuteronomy 24:15 – Paying wages on time

Applies to Jewish people doing agriculture in the land of Israel and, in principle, to both Jews and God-fearing Gentile believers in every time and place.

- P122 – Deuteronomy 24:19 – Leaving forgotten sheaves for the poor
- N214 – Deuteronomy 24:19 – Not returning for a forgotten sheaf or forgotten fruits

Applies to Jewish men in general, but the prohibition is also incumbent upon the widow herself. The prohibition applies in every place and time until the matter is legally resolved.

- N357 – Deuteronomy 25:5 – Not marrying or engaging in sexual relations with a woman obligated to a Levirate marriage

Applies to Jewish husbands (and possibly the God-fearing Gentile) in a time and place where Torah courts held civil authority.

- N359 – Deuteronomy 22:19 – Not divorcing a bride that one has slandered
- P219 – Deuteronomy 22:19 – Keeping the law concerning a man who defames his bride

Applies to Jewish soldiers in the army of the Lord at a time when the Jewish people occupy their land, but the principles apply universally.

- P221 – Deuteronomy 21:11 – Following the procedure of the beautiful captive woman
- N263 – Deuteronomy 21:14 – Not selling a captive woman
- N264 – Deuteronomy 21:14 – Not enslaving a captive woman

Applies to judges and agents of a Jewish court of law in every place when the Sanhedrin holds civil authority.

- P224 – Deuteronomy 25:2 – Administering the punishment of flogging
- N300 – Deuteronomy 25:3 – Not exceeding the appropriate number of lashes

Applies to the Jewish people and God-fearing Gentiles in Jerusalem with the Sanctuary and Levitical system in place.

- N155 – Deuteronomy 23:21 – Not delaying payment of vows
- N100 – Deuteronomy 23:18 – Not bringing the hire of a harlot or the price of a dog into the temple

Applies to eunuchs in every time and place.

- N360 – Deuteronomy 23:1 – A eunuch may not marry a Jewish woman

Applies to both Jews and God-fearing Gentile believers struck with biblical leprosy, but only in a time and place where a certified and competent priest can diagnose the malady.

- N308 – Deuteronomy 24:8 – Not concealing the physical signs of leprosy

Applies to government and military authorities in the land of Israel when the Jewish people occupy the land.

- N311 – Deuteronomy 24:5 – Not taking the bridegroom away from home for the first year

Applies to Jewish (and possibly the God-fearing Gentile) farmers doing agriculture in the land of Israel.

- P201 – Deuteronomy 23:24 – Allowing a hired worker to eat from the produce he is hired to work

Applies to Jewish judges on a court of law and, in principle, to all judges in every time and place.

- N287 – Deuteronomy 24:16 – Not accepting testimony from relatives

Applies to the Jewish people and God-fearing Gentile believers in the land of Israel.

- N254 – Deuteronomy 23:15 – Not returning a fugitive slave to his master

Applies to the judges of the Sanhedrin in Jerusalem when the Sanhedrin has civil authority

- P230 – Deuteronomy 21:22 – Hanging the corpses of certain convicts after their execution

Applies to the judges of the Sanhedrin and incumbents in the land of Israel when the Sanhedrin wields civil authority.

- P229 – Deuteronomy 22:24 – The Sanhedrin must administer the death penalty of stoning

Applies to the judges on a Jewish court in every time and place.

- P217 – Deuteronomy 25:9 – Performing the ritual of *chalitzah*

CHAPTER 8

When You Enter

"Ki Tavo"
Deuteronomy 26:1–29:8

Ki Tavo, meaning, "When you enter," is the fiftieth reading of the Torah. The parsha begins with the laws regarding the firstfruits and the tithe presentation. Chapter 27 discusses the idea of placing stones as a visual reminder of the great things God has done. There is extensive text reiterating the curses and the blessing in chapter 28. The latter half of chapter 28 expounds the curses, rebukes, and consequences that would follow disobedience including famine, poverty, and illness. Ki Tavo is a tough parsha to read, as there is four times more Scripture covering the curses than the blessing. The parsha concludes with Moses telling the Israelites that they now have a heart to know, eyes to see, ears to hear, and the ability to recognize God's great signs and wonders they have seen for the last forty years (29:4).

Firstfruits (Bikkurim)

Moses begins by reminding the Israelites of the laws regarding the firstfruits (Exodus 23:19). Deuteronomy 26 contains the details of the offering. Falling on the heels of Passover as the Israelites celebrated their freedom from Egypt, God commanded them to bring an omer[176] of their firstfruits

---

[176] An *omer* is about one quart.

to the priest (Leviticus 23:11). The firstfruits referred specifically to the seven species of fruit of the Promised Land—wheat, barley, grapes, figs, pomegranates, olives, and dates—but probably would have been an omer of barley as it would be the first to harvest. The offering of the firstfruits is also known as Easter by the Christian community. The rabbit and the egg symbolize fertility and new birth; in the same way, the firstfruits of the Torah celebrate the fertility of the land. As soon as a Jewish farmer would see the first fruit in the field, he would tie a string around it and declare it *bikkurim*.[177]As soon as that first fruit ripened, he would bring an omer of it to the temple. The priest was then to wave that offering before God to gain favor for the children of Israel. The giver of the bikkurim would then recite the Scripture from Deuteronomy 26:5–10 and leave an offering for the priest. By doing so, he was dedicating everything he had to the service of God, one of the goals of creation.[178] The anticipation of a bountiful harvest was the expectation. After the first fruit was given to God, the crops could be harvested. In 1 Corinthians 15:20–23, Paul identifies Jesus as the first fruit of those who will be raised from the dead. In the same way that the offering of the firstfruits would indicate a faith and anticipation of more to come in the harvest, the resurrection of Jesus, as the firstfruits would anticipate the resurrection of the believer.

Counting the Omer

The giving of the first fruit was to be followed by joyous celebration. The offering of the firstfruits is when the Israelites would begin to "count the omer." Counting the omer is known in Hebrew as *sefriat ha'omer*. An omer is a unit of measure equivalent to about 2.3 quarts or 2.2 liters.

According to the Torah (Leviticus. 23:15), it is a commandment to count the days from Passover to Shavu'ot. Every night, the Jew is to recite a blessing and state the count of the omer in both weeks and days. For example, on the tenth day, one is to say, "Today is ten days, which is one

[177] Dr. D. K. Olukoya. *The Mystery of First Fruit Offering*, Kindle ed. Sabo-Yaba: The Battle Cry Christian Ministries, 2007. Kindle location 290.
[178] Scherman. *Chumash*, 2000, 1068.

week and three days of the omer." Daily they would give thanks for all the provisions and mercy of God.[179]

As they counted the omer, it was a time of devoting oneself to the service of God. Thomas Aquinas declares that devotion has particularly meritorious character in its "will to give oneself promptly to those things which pertain to God's services" as when giving the offering of the first-fruits. Therefore, he derives that devotion is a special act of the will.[180]

The Sadducees interpreted Leviticus 23:11 to mean the omer count was to begin the Sabbath during the Feast of Unleavened Bread, but the Pharisees interpreted it to be the Sabbath at the beginning of the Festival of Unleavened Bread.[181] This means that the Sadducees' omer count would always begin on a Sunday, and the Pharisees would begin the omer count on the sixteenth of Aviv and end on the sixth of Sivan.[182] For the messianic Jews, much of the debate surrounding the dates of the omer count surrounds calculating and recalculating the second coming of Christ,[183] although most messianic Jews follow the interpretation of the Pharisees.[184]

Tithes

Following the details of bikkurim (the firstfruits), Moses gives more details about the various tithes. The Israelite was to take a formal vow (Deuteronomy 26:13–14) declaring that he had given his tithe. Every three years, any undistributed offerings were to be made *(viui ma'aser)*. The farmer then would ask God to bless his land for a plentiful harvest.

The Israelite was to tithe one tenth of the harvest for the priest and the Levites. An additional one tenth of the harvest was to be set aside each year for

[179] Jewish Holidays: Lag b'Omer & Counting of the Omer. http://www.jewishvirtuallibrary.org/jsource/Judaism/holidayb.html (accessed May 20, 2014).
[180] St. Thomas Aquinas. *On Prayer and the Contemplative Life,* Kindle ed. Public Domain Books, 2009. Kindle location 619.
[181] Huey. *Counting the Omer,* 2011. Kindle location 186.
[182] Jeffrey H. Tigay. *JPS Torah Commentary: Deuteronomy.* Philadelphia: Jewish Publication Society, 1996, 157. Quoted in William Mark Huey, *Counting the Omer: A Daily Devotional toward Shavu'ot,* Kindle ed. Richardson: TNN Press, 2011.
[183] Huey. *Counting the Omer,* 2011. Kindle location 251.
[184] Ibid., 218.

the sanctuary to use during the holidays, and in the third and sixth years in the sabbatical cycle, they were to be given to the poor, the widow, the orphan, and the proselyte. The fruitfulness of the land was dependent on the tithe for the poor, making it most important. Jewish tradition states that charity is one of the three things believed to get one's name written in the Book of Life.

The different types of tithes listed in the Torah include the *Terumah*, the *pe'ah*, the *ma'aser behemah, ma'aser rishon, ma'aser shini, ma'aser ani*, and *ma'aser kesafim*.

After harvesting all crops, one fifth was to be given as Terumah to the priest. The edges of all crops were to be left as Terumah for the poor to glean (Leviticus 19:9) as the pe'ah tithe. The ma'aser behemah tithe pertains to the kosher cattle: one tenth of these cattle were to be offered at the sanctuary. The ma'aser rishon is the tenth of the produce given to the Levite. The ma'aser sheni is the portion that would be eaten at the celebration in the third and sixth years of the *shemittah* (the seven-year sabbatical cycle), and the ma'aser ani is the portion the poor would eat in those years. The ma'aser kesafim refers to one tenth of one's money earned that was to be given to charity.

There is disagreement among the rabbinic scholars as to whether or not the tithes should continue in the absence of the official temple. First, the part of the tithes that would be eaten by the priest or Levite could only be eaten if they were ritually clean. Without the ashes of the red heifer, a priest cannot be clean. Second, there is doubt about the reliability of status of the priest and Levites who live today. That being said, today's practice is to take some of the tithes but not eat them. Rather, they are disposed of in a respectable manner.[185]

One misconception regularly heard is that the tithes and offerings that the Israelites needed to make were such a burden and caused great hardship yet were necessary in order to assure their salvation. However, salvation for Jews was and is based on the grace of God as extended to Israel. They were saved merely because they were Jews. The blessings and curses, on the other hand, had everything to do with obedience.

---

[185] Rabbi Bradley Shavit Artson and Rabbi Patricia Fenton. *"Mitzvot Ha-Teluyot Ba'aretz." Walking with God.* U8:5-6. http://ziegler.aju.edu/default.aspx?id=5188 (accessed May 19, 2014).

Blessings and Curses

As Moses drew near to the end of his life, his opportunities to influence the younger generation of the wilderness grew slim. He spelled out the blessing of obedience and then unpacked the consequences of sin. The rebuke, ninety-eight curses in all, seems endless. The Hebrew word for "bless" is *barakh*, which means to bestow favor and protection, while the Hebrew word used for "curse" is *arar*, meaning to snare, bind, or be damned. *Arar* is an antonym for *barakh*.

This section of Torah might cause one to skip ahead a few chapters. Denial can seem warm compared to the wrath of God as shouted across the valley between Mount Gerizim and Mount Ebal; however, there was more to this event than merely instilling the fear of God in the children of Israel.

None of this generation of people were with Moses at the giving and accepting of the Torah forty years earlier, so this was to be like a second birth, a new covenant with the younger generation. This would be a chance for them to publicly accept the Torah upon entering the Promised Land in the same way their fathers did at Mount Sinai. Moses instructed them to inscribe on stones the Torah "clearly." Sages say that *clearly* means "in every language" that was spoken at the time, citing a miraculous feat to inscribe them in all seventy languages[186] (See Genesis 10–11).

Moses divided the tribes into three groups; six tribes he sent to the top of Mount Gerizim to represent the blessing, and six to the top of Mount Ebal to represent the curses, while the ark, the priest, and the elders of the Levites stood in the valley of Shechem below. The elders of the Levites shouted out the blessing and the curses, to which the tribes responded with "Amen."

According to Talmud, as Ezra was dividing Torah into portions, it was decided to read the curses in Leviticus before Shavu'ot; then before Rosh Hashanah, the curses from Deuteronomy would be read. This was "so that the year and its curses can conclude."[187]

---

[186] A. Cohen. *Soncino Babylonian Talmud Sotah* 32a, Kindle ed. Teaneck: Talmudic Books, 2012. Kindle location 5909.

[187] Maurice Simon and Moses Hirsch Segal. Soncino Babylonian Talmud Megillah and*Shekalim*. 31b, Kindle ed. Teaneck: Talmudic Books, 2012. Kindle location 5451.

Deuteronomy 27:9 tells us that people of Israel belong to God. One should not interpret this as a mere acquaintance: the Israelites were to be the family of God. This implies a relationship that is personal and intimate like a married couple or father and son,[188] making obedience and respect a priority. A parent would not forget his or her own child's favorite toy, and a wife would not forget her own husband's favorite food; in the same respect, the child of God should not forget what pleases Him.

Moses' Final Charge to the Israelites

Moses' final charge to the Israelites is all about remembering. Again, this common theme appears repeatedly in Deuteronomy. Moses reminds them what God did to Pharaoh, as well as who gave the Reubenite, the Gadite, and the half tribe of Manasseh the towns of Heshbon and Bashan. Moses implores them to open their eyes, their hearts, and their ears to behold the marvelous things of the Lord. The parsha ends with an encouraging note and reiteration from the Shema. "You shall observe the words of this covenant, and you shall preform them, so that you will succeed in all you do."

The New Jerusalem

The reading from the Haftarah for Ki Tavo also offers much encouragement as it gives a picture of the New Jerusalem (Isaiah 60:1–2). Thousands of books have been written about the New Jerusalem that John describes in the book of Revelation, and all of the literature reveals the freedom that will be found when the Messiah, Jesus Christ, returns for His church. Isaiah paints a beautiful description of the Light of the World. Here he describes a kingdom without a need for artificial light because the city is the light of God. This is the paradise where all of Israel will be saved. It is the final Promised Land that includes the restoration and the glory of Israel (Romans 11:25–36).

Salvation is of the Lord (Micah 7:7) and not because of anything we have done but rather because of God's great mercy (Titus 3:5). We escape the curses of the law because of what Jesus did for us on the cross. He is

---

[188] Block. *How I Love Your Torah*, 2011, 151.

the "Lamb of God who takes away the sin of the world" (John 1:29). In the same way that a married person is released from the bonds of marriage when a spouse dies, so we are free from the bonds of sin because of the death of our Messiah. The believer is no longer "under the law" (Romans 6:14). We have now been released from the bondage of the law so that we are free to serve in newness of the Spirit and not in oldness of the law (Romans 7:6), so we can be obedient to the meaning of the Torah. We are free to serve and obey in the joy of the Spirit.

Mitzvot[189]

Applies to Jews and God-fearing Gentiles in every time and place.

- P8 – Deuteronomy 26:17 – Walking in God's ways

Applies to Jewish people doing agriculture in the land of Israel with the temple and Levitical system in place.

- P132 – Deuteronomy 26:5 – Contains the law pertaining to the Scripture to be recited when bringing in the Firstfruits
- P131 – Deuteronomy 26:13 – The avowal of the tithe
- P152 – Deuteronomy 26:14 – Not spending the *tameh*, second tithe redemption money, except on food and drink

Applies to Jews and God-fearing Gentiles in Jerusalem with the temple and Levitical system in place.

- P151 – Deuteronomy 26:14 – Not eating the *tameh*, second tithe while morning
- P150 – Deuteronomy 26:14 – Not eating an unredeemed *tameh*, second tithe

---

[189] Numbered by Rambam. Grouped by applicability according to First Fruits of Zion.

CHAPTER 9

Standing

"Nitzavim"
Deuteronomy 29:9–30:20

Parsha Nitzavim, the fifty-first reading from the Torah, is the beginning of Moses' final appeal to the Israelites. The title, Nitzavim, comes from the first verse of the parsha "You stand *(nitzavim)* today, all of you, before the LORD your God." There are no specific laws in this parsha; instead, Moses implores those he has spent the last forty years with to obey the entire covenant. His final warnings include the consequences for when they do fail. He prophetically tells them about their future exile, as well as the redemption that will follow. He also tells them of their repentance. Moses describes a time when all the people will ask why they have been exiled from the land God swore to their ancestors to give them. The reading of this parsha is the Shabbat before Rosh Hashanah, so Jewish tradition calls Deuteronomy 30 *HaTashuvah* (The Chapter of Repentance). Moses was so concerned about the continuity of the Torah that not only did he speak to the Israelites, but he also addressed the chiefs, elders, young, and old. He specifically lets the women and the foreigners know that they also are included in this final charge. He makes a point to call everyone, great and small, in that no one is insignificant or unfit for the Torah.

> "You stand today, all of you, before the LORD your God:
> your chiefs, your tribes, your elders and your officers, *even*
> all the men of Israel, your little ones, your wives, and the

alien who is within your camps, from the one who chops
your wood to the one who draws your water, that you may
enter into the covenant with the LORD your God, and into
His oath which the LORD your God is making with you
today, in order that He may establish you today as His
people and that He may be your God, just as He spoke to
you and as He swore to your fathers, to Abraham, Isaac,
and Jacob."   —Deuteronomy 29:10–13

In fact, in verse 15, he addresses the future generations. "And for those
who are not here with us today." There is no disclaimer here stating that
the Americans are exempt, that the Gentiles need not bother, or that the
women can turn away from God if life gets too tough. Every person of
every generation and every generation to come is included, particularly the
foreigner who comes from a distant land.

Moses emphasizes the accessibility of the Torah, insisting that although it seems impossible to know the Torah and obey the Torah, it is not
beyond their ability to achieve. He tells the people the Torah is not across
a sea or in heaven where no person can reach it: the Torah can be found,
Moses says, "in your mouth and in your hearts" (30:14) if they only make
a sincere effort to grasp hold of it.[190] Before they reach to grasp hold of it,
however, they must make a choice to do so.

Freedom of Choice

Most commentators of old as well as contemporary scholars will agree that
Deuteronomy 30:15–20 represent the thrust of the entire Torah.

See, I have set before you today life and prosperity, and
death and adversity; in that I command you today to love
the Lord your God, to walk in His ways and to keep His
commandments and His statutes and His judgments, that
you may live and multiply, and that the Lord your God
may bless you in the land where you are entering to possess

---

[190] Scherman. *Chumash,* 2000, 1092.

it. But if your heart turns away and you will not obey, but are drawn away and worship other gods and serve them, I declare to you today that you shall surely perish. You will not prolong your days in the land where you are crossing the Jordan to enter and possess it. I call heaven and earth to witness against you today, that I have set before you life and death, the blessing and the curse. So choose life in order that you may live, you and your descendants, by loving the Lord your God, by obeying His voice, and by holding fast to Him; for this is your life and the length of your days, that you may live in the land which the Lord swore to your fathers, to Abraham, Isaac, and Jacob, to give them.

This reading is from the NASB translation, which I personally find to be the most accurate, literal, and easy-to-read translation; however, I'm not sure I agree with the use of the English word "prosperity" in verse 1. The Hebrew word translated as prosperity is *towb*. According to the Strong's definition, it means "good" in the widest sense, encompassing cheerful, at ease, best, better, gracious, beautiful, joyful, favor, fine, merry, pleasant, ready, and sweet, as well as prosperous and wealth. The word towb appears in the Old Testament 562 times. We see it used every time God created in Genesis and He saw that it was towb. Towb was used to describe the beauty of Rebekah in Genesis 24:1, the towb old age in which Abraham died (25:8), and the towb rejoicing of the Lord (Deuteronomy 30:9). Whereas the English word *prosperity* has connotations of being rich or having more money than one could spend, this verse is often used in the deceiving "prosperity gospel" of today. I, however, believe that in the context of Moses' final plea to the children of Israel, it had to do with choices they would make for the rest of their lives. Moses laid it out for them: choose life and the towb, or death and evil. This implies a choice as a deliberate action as opposed to a social status by which they might happen to live. Moses implored them to choose to learn the Torah, live it out, and teach it to their children. This is a core principle of the Shema, the prayer recited twice daily by the Jews. Joshua knew this choice (Joshua 24:15), and so did Ezra (7:10). The choice is between the Torah and that which is utterly opposed to Torah: death.[191]

Since the beginning of time, life has been about choice and consequences. In the garden of Eden, much was good and pleasurable. There was only one tree of which Adam and Eve were not to eat the fruit. They had a choice to make: God's way or the way of evil. God even told them what to choose (Genesis 2:16), yet they still chose poorly. There are still choices that Christians need to make as well. We are free to choose a life of obedience with all the rewards that go along with it or a life of rebellion and the consequences that will follow. This freedom to choose is given to all of humanity. That is freedom to be saved, of which Luther declares, "From these considerations any one may clearly see how a Christian man is free from all things; so that he needs no works in order to be justified and saved, but receives these gifts in abundance from faith alone."[192]

Geisler devotes ten pages to listing the church Fathers who would agree.[193] Scriptures call us to choose good over evil. Micah declares, "Do justice, love kindness, and walk humbly with God" (Micah 6:8). According to the words of Micah, one needs to make a deliberate choice.

The sages call the Torah the "tree of life" based on Proverbs 3:18. "She is a tree of life to those who take hold of her and happy are all who hold her fast." Although, in Proverbs 3:18, the "she" is referring to wisdom, traditional Judaism identifies the study of Torah as the tree of life (*etz chaim*). Etz chaim refers to the two wooden poles that hold a Torah scroll. Every Shabbat after the reading of the Torah, as it is placed back into the ark, a hymn is sung called the Etz Chaim. The inference here is that the Word of God is the tree of life, and Jesus, the Word of God made flesh (John 1), is the way and the life (John 14:6). The reason Jesus came is so that all may have life (John 10:10).

The text of the Haftarah (Isaiah 61:10–63:9) is the seventh and final Haftarah of Consolation. These seven Haftarah portions begin on the Shabbat following Tisha b'Av and continue until the Shabbat before Rosh

---

[191] Scherman. *Chumash*, 2000, 1093.

[192] Martin Luther. *Concerning Christian Liberty*, Kindle ed. Public Domain Books, 2006. Kindle location 329.

[193] Norman L. Geisler. *Chosen but Free: A Balanced View of Divine Election*. Minneapolis: Bethany House Publishers, 2001, 150–159.

Hashanah. Isaiah begins by describing the joy of salvation as the fruit of their labors spread to all the nations. Therefore, Isaiah proclaims God's words, saying, "For Zion's sake, I will not be silent, and for Jerusalem's sake, I will not be still." God will not passively sit by and wait for redemption, rather, He will sow the seeds, harvest the crops, and clean the way, until His name is known to the ends of the earth. The Haftarah ends with a verse that reveals God's empathy for the suffering of His people. "In all their troubles, He was troubled," and an angel from before Him saved them" (63:9). Though the Haftarah does not contain an explicit reference to the Torah portion, it does describe the future redemption, and as the holiday of Rosh Hashanah is approaching, the thrust of these Scriptures is inspirational.

During the reading of Nitzavim, the Jewish people are seriously considering where they will spend eternity. Paul quotes Deuteronomy 30:11–14 as he recalls, "The Word is near you, in your mouth and in your heart" (Romans 10:5–8). Paul states that the Word is faith, confessed with the mouth, and believed in the heart, resulting in righteousness and salvation. He insists that whoever believes, whoever calls on God, will be saved. Choice is for all humankind. The examples are many from Genesis to Revelation; wide is the way that leads to destruction, and narrow is the gate that leads to life (Matthew 7:13–14). Six thousand years ago, Adam and Eve chose to eat the fruit; two thousand years ago, the people chose Barabbas (Matthew 27:21). Keeping an eternal perspective, life and freedom lay in the balance of choice. Choose wisely; choose today: whom shall you serve? God chose all Christians to be priest, a chosen race for His own possession (1 Peter 2:9). The call to priestly duty is not just a blessing; it requires responsibility. For the Christian, being grafted in has purpose greater than the mere enjoyment of blessings; there is a ministry to perform and life to choose.[194] In the day of Moses, more was expected of the priests, and less was given. They were teachers and guardians of moral life and were warned to live uprightly.[195] It is unfortunate that this righteous living has been lost by most in the church today as the emphasis is put on privilege.

---

[194] David M. Levy. *The Tabernacle: Shadows of the Messiah: Its Sacrifices, Services, and Priesthood*. Grand Rapids: Kregel Publications, 2003, 143.

[195] Jeffery Enoch Feinberg. *Walk Genesis! A Messianic Jewish Devotional Commentary for Readers of the Torah, Haftarah, and B'rit Chadashah*. Clarksville: Lederer Books, a division of Messianic Jewish Publishers, 1998, 114.

Freedom of Will

There is no shortage of literature about man's freedom relating to his salvation. The rift between the Christian views of predestination has grown deeper and wider. Akiba, known to defend the divine predestination of the Jewish people, argues emphatically on freedom of will, to which he allows no limitations, and calls total depravity an excuse for sin. Some believe this view is in direct opposition to Christianity's doctrine of grace, which leaves many unaccountable.[196]

Philo speaks of slavery of two kinds: physical slavery and slavery of the soul. Philo determines that man is the master of the body but wickedness and passion control the soul. To be free physically is to be fearless of what another human can do to the body while being free spiritually is to have peace of mind. Philo looks deeper into the character of the man who is truly free and determines he is the man who makes God his leader.[197] According to Jukes, this should take us farther to seek to be conformed to Him, so "that which are true for us in Him, may be made true in our soul's experience by the Spirit."[198]

---

[196] JewishEncyclopedia.com, sv "Akiba Ben Joseph," http://www.jewishencyclopedia.com/articles/1033-akiba-ben-joseph (accessed April 19, 2014).

[197] Yong. *Every Good Man Is Free,* 2013. Kindle location 28604.

[198] Andrew Jukes. *The Law of the Offerings,* Kindle ed. Counted Faithful, 2012. Kindle location 1970.

CHAPTER 10

And He Went

"Vayeilech"
Deuteronomy 31

The fifty-fifth reading from the Torah, Vayeilech *(and he went)*, is read with Nitzavim most years and always right before Rosh Hashanah and *The Days of Awe*. The parsha begins with "Moses went and spoke these words to all of Israel." The text then says, "I am 120 years old today." This day was Moses' birthday and, according to the Chumash, the last day of his life.[199] Scholars place this day as 7 Adar.[200]

Moses knows that after he dies, the people will rebel once again; thus, he encourages the people and Joshua to be strong and courageous. Moses insisted that Joshua and the people look to the Lord for guidance. Moses stressed that the Lord was the leader of the people. Moses commands that the children of Israel assemble every seven years to renew their covenant with God and publicly read the Torah during the Sukkot festival. This public reading, called the *Hakhel*, is taken from Deuteronomy 31:9–13. After turning the leadership over to Joshua, Moses handed his copy of the Torah to the Levites. Moses then instructed the Levites to place the Torah next to the *Aron HaKodesh* (ark of the covenant).

---

[199] Scherman, Rashi. *Chumash*, 2000, 1094.
[200] Tracey R. Rich. *Judaism 101*. http://www.jewfaq.org/moshe.htm (accessed May 20, 2014).

Read the Torah—Hakhel

We are told that faith comes from hearing the Word (Romans 10:17). This was not a new concept for the apostle Paul. The mitzvah numbered P16 is based on Deuteronomy 31:12. There is little doubt that Paul was referring to this law when he was writing the text of Romans.

Once every seven years, during Sukkot, the nation was commanded to come together at the temple to hear the Torah read aloud (*Hakhel* means "gathering"). This command ensured they would hear, learn, and fear the Lord and be careful to observe all the words of the Law (31:12). It is not clear from the text as to the meaning of "this Law," but most would agree it is the reading of the book of Deuteronomy, although it is not impossible to read all five books of Moses in a week. In fact, in the English language, it would only take about fifteen hours for the average reader to read the Torah in its entirety. The book of Deuteronomy, on the other hand, would take less than three or four hours for that same reader. Verse 13 adds an additional reason for listening to the Torah: so the children who do not know will hear and learn.

Everyone is to attend the Hakhel, even the foreigner. Although the stranger would not be bound by the Law as the Jewish men and women, the hope would be that the foreigner might be inspired to convert.[201] According to the Chumash, Jews will never force or even encourage conversion, but they are to live in a manner that will honor God and will be inspiring to the foreigner.[202] This is a great example of how the life of a Christian should look desirable to the nonbeliever. How many nonbelievers will want to hear the plan of salvation if the Christian appears stressed, crabby, and miserable?

Hester Panim

Deuteronomy 31:17 is, no doubt, some tough Scripture to read. *Hester panim* is the concept of God hiding His face. My first thought was to skip this concept because the whole idea of God hiding from those He loves

---

[201] Scherman, Ibn Ezra. *Chumash,* 2000, 1096.
[202] Scherman. *Chumash,* 2000, 1097.

sounds like hell, and it begged the question "Where is the freedom in that?" I was moderately afraid there would be no freedom to be found in hester panim. Yet Scripture repeatedly reveals that good can come from affliction (Psalm 119:71).

Hester panim is not only an Old Testament concept. We read about it in Romans 1:28. "And just as they did not see fit to acknowledge God any longer, God gave them over to a depraved mind ..." Isaiah writes about hester panim, telling all to seek the Lord before it is too late (Isaiah 55:6). According to the apostle Paul, the absence of God's presence can be the reason one goes looking for it. Paul believed that hester panim (the sorrow that is according to the will of God) produces repentance without regret, leading one to salvation and producing zeal and eager pursuit for justice (2 Corinthians 7:10–11).

Still, to think that God would "forsake" one He created for non-compliance seems so final. However, a closer examination of the Hebrew word used in Deuteronomy 31:17 indicates that God has not abandoned them. The word *azab* is translated as "forsake." This means to loosen or to relinquish, permit, fortify, and help. It has the meaning of absence, not emptiness. It is not a final act of God; it is an action, a process as opposed to a completed state of God. It has been referred to as *the Eclipse of God*. This is a great visual, as one knows that an eclipse is not the absence of the moon or the sun; it is merely obscured, and it is momentary. Jewish tradition would say the presence of God is hiding (present), not hidden and final. According to David Wolpe, hester panim is a profound way of suggesting how deeply faith can feel that God's presence has fled from humanity.[203] It seems to be more consistent with God's character to say hester panim is more of God's reaction to evil, brought on by the evil of the human heart and actions, as opposed to God's way of oppressing humankind. God can have nothing to do with evil—why would he want to look at it? Hester panim is an expression of God's empathy over the suffering of the innocent.[204]

---

[203] David Wolpe. *Hester Panim in Modern Jewish Thought*. Modern Judaism 17.1. The Johns Hopkins University Press, 1997, 25–26.

[204] Rabbi Ute Steyer, MA. "A Different Interpretation of Hester Panim," *The Jewish Theological Seminary*.

Considering that ultimate freedom comes from salvation, who would want to be left alone to flounder? If hester panim would bring one to repentance and thus salvation, then hester panim could be described as an action of God freeing those He loves from the bondage of sin. James said, "Draw near to God and He will draw near to you" (James 4:8). It seems appropriate, then, to read about hester panim as the Days of Awe approach. This would be the right time to seek God's face and His forgiveness.

Writing the Torah

Although this command applies only to the Jewish men, this does not imply that it cannot be fulfilled by anyone else who finds it beneficial. The commandment is designed to encourage one to love and remember God at all times. What better way to remember God's Word than to write out the Torah in one's own hand?[205]

The Haftarah portion read with Vayeilech includes Hosea 14:2–10, Joel 2:11–27, and Micah 7:18–20. These prophetic Scriptures follow the same theme, calling for repentance. Hosea cries out, "Take these words with you and return to the Lord." Joel calls the children of Israel to assemble and seek forgiveness. Micah then reminds them of God's faithfulness to restore Israel after their repentance. During the years that Vayeilech falls on Shabbat Shuvah, the Shabbat between Rosh Hashanah and Yom Kippur, a portion from Isaiah is read, 55:6–8.

> Seek the LORD while He may be found;
> Call upon Him while He is near.
> Let the wicked forsake his way
> And the unrighteous man his thoughts;
> And let him return to the LORD,
> And He will have compassion on him,
> And to our God,
> For He will abundantly pardon.
> "For My thoughts are not your thoughts,
> Nor are your ways My ways," declares the LORD.

---

[205] Brauner. 613 *Commandments in Prose*, 2012, 3.

Rosh Hashanah

Rosh Hashanah, also known as the Feast of Trumpets, is celebrated on 1 and 2 Tishrei on the Jewish calendar. Rosh Hashanah literally means the "head of the year" and is an important day in the Jewish year. This is the day of new beginnings, a chance to commit to better thoughts, better intentions, and better deeds. Rosh Hashanah is the beginning of a period known as the Days of Awe. Jews will celebrate Rosh Hashanah with much joy for two days in both Israel and the Diaspora. Talmudic sages describe the two days of the New Year as Yoma Arichtahin Aramaic, meaning "one long day."

Preparation for this day starts a month prior on the second of Elul with the daily blowing of the shofar, which is a ram's horn that sounds much like a trumpet. Listening to the sound of the shofar is the climax of Rosh Hashanah. The Torah does not specifically state why the shofar should be blown or why this day is called Yom Tru'a ("a day of shofar blowing"), but Rambam suggested that it is a "wake-up call" to remind us of our Creator; it initiates a moment in which we can consider ways to improve ourselves.[206]

The Tru'a is a specific assembly of blasts starting with *tekiah*, a long, single blast, followed by *byshevarim*, three shorts blasts, followed by several short blasts to awaken the soul called *teruah*, and one final long blast called *tekiah hagadol*.

Special prayers of forgiveness called Slixot are recited daily. The Slixot prayers help the worshipers focus their minds on repentance for themselves and for the people of Israel. This is when the Jews examine their behavior in the last year and seek forgiveness from God, at the same time promising to improve their behavior in the next year. The Jews believe that the way you meet the first day of the New Year sets the tone for the entire year: if you are joyful and at peace on Rosh Hashanah, the rest of the year will be peaceful and joyful as well.

This holiday is not comparable to the New Year's celebrations in

---

[206] Dovid Rosenfeld. *Maimonides on Life: Hanging in the Balance, Part II.* Hil. Teshuvah 3:4, 2001. http://www.torah.org/learning/mlife/LORch3-4b.html (accessed May 20, 2014).

America, however. Celebrations may include symbolic foods, such as apples dipped in honey for a sweet year or pomegranate seeds to ensure a fruitful year. What it does not include is drinking oneself into a stupor or making thoughtless declarations that only last two weeks into the New Year.

The binding of Isaac is a major theme on Rosh Hashanah. According to Jewish tradition, God told Abraham that the shofar is to be blown on Rosh Hashanah to remind the people of the substitutionary sacrifice the Lord provided.[207] As Rambam puts it, "The shofar calls out: 'Awake, you sleepers, from your sleep! Arise, you slumberers from your slumber! Repent with contrition! Remember your Creator! ... Peer into your souls, improve your ways and your deeds ... '"[208]

Preparing for Rosh Hashanah traditionally involves three types of teshuva: turning to God, turning to those one has harmed to ask forgiveness, and turning to those in need by giving charity. The idea is that if the adequate teshuva has been done, one will find *tova umetuka*, a sweet and peaceful new year. How much more should those who believe in the greater sacrifice of Jesus as the Lamb of God celebrate this day? Rosh Hashanah can be a "sanctified reminder" of God's authority in the lives of the believers. As Christians, one is commanded to watch and be ready for His upcoming appearance. One therefore ought to be in a constant state of teshuva, for "He has told you, O man, what is good; and what does the Lord require of you but to do justice, to love kindness, and to walk humbly with your God?" (Micah 6:8).

---

[207] John Parsons. *Teshuvah and Creation*. Hebrew for Christians (accessed May 20, 2014). http://hebrew4christians.com/Holidays/Fall_Holidays/Elul/Creation/creation.html.

[208] Dovid Rosenfeld. *Maimonides on Life: Hanging in the Balance, Part II.* (Hil. Teshuvah 3:4, 2001. http://www.torah.org/learning/mlife/LORch3-4b.html (accessed May 20 2014).

Mitzvot[209]

Applies to the king of Israel with the temple and Levitical system in place when the people are in the land.

- P16 – Deuteronomy 31:12 – Hakhel during Sukkos - Assembling every seventh year to hear the Torah read

Applies to Jewish men in every time and place.

- P18 – Deuteronomy 31:19 – Writing a copy of the Torah

---

[209] Numbered by Rambam. Grouped by applicability according to First Fruits of Zion.

CHAPTER 11

Give Ear

"Ha'azinu"
Deuteronomy 32:1–52

The date is Adar 7 and the children of Israel are assembled on the plains of Moab, just outside the Promised Land. It is Moses' birthday and the last day of his life. God speaks to Moses, telling him what to say to the Israelite people. The word *Ha'azinu* literally means, "Give ear," which means, "Listen to this." Ha'azinu is the fifty-third reading from the Torah and the first word of the Song of Moses, which begins with the words "Give ear (ha'azinu), O heavens, and let me speak" (Deuteronomy 32:1).[210]

Ha'azinu is the shortest parsha; only a single chapter long, it mainly consists of the Song of Moses that we read about in chapter 31. The Song of Moses is a prophetic vision warning Israel about its future apostasy and the resulting wrath of God. Moses called on heaven and earth to give testimony to the misfortunes that would follow if Israel sins and the ultimate joy that will come with the final redemption. The song looks to the future, even envisioning the messianic arrival with alarming apocalyptic imagery. The Lord told Moses to write the song, teach it, and put it on their lips, and Moses did so that same day. After the conclusion of the song, Moses is told to climb Mount Nebo to view the Promised Land from the distance. This happened the same day that Moses died.

---

[210] Boaz, Michael. First Fruits of Zion. *Ha'azinu.* http://torahportions.org/this-portion.html?portion=Ha'azinu (accessed May 20, 2014).

Ha'azinu is one of only two songs that Moses wrote. The other song is The Song of the Sea in Exodus 15.

The Song of Moses

The parsha begins with Deuteronomy 32:1–2

> Give ear, O heavens, and let me speak; and let the earth hear the words of my mouth. Let my teaching drop as the rain, my speech distill as the dew, as the droplets on the fresh grass and as the showers on the herb.

The song involves five historical themes.

1. God created the world so all nations would be involved in accomplishing the will of God.
2. The people rebelled, even after God gave them the land.
3. While they deserved death for their sin, God's mercy and grace brought them exile.
4. This gave them the promise that one day they would be redeemed.
5. And Moses described these future events in his song.[211]

Essentially, parsha Ha'azinu is about Israel's history: past, present, and future. Starting with the creation of the formation of the seventy nations (Genesis 10, Deuteronomy 32:7–8), the parsha delves into the kindness God has shown the children of Israel. God found them in the wilderness and protected them as the eagle would protect their babes under their wings.

Moses' song explores the unity between heaven and earth. Moses establishes the similarities between the rain that comes from heaven and the Torah that also comes from heaven. In the same respect that the rain falls from heaven and feeds the plants of the earth, so the Torah would feed the soul of all those who read it. Similarly, the dew is a result of the rain and remains long after the rain stops to provide further nourishment. There is

---

[211] Scherman, Sforno. *Chumash*, 2000, 1101.

correlation here to the Talmud and Mishnah, which are a recapitulation of the Torah. Sforno articulates that for the wise, the Torah would come like pelting rain, while for the younger or those only capable of understanding small parts of the Torah, wisdom comes like the dew.[212] Rashi also taught that like the storm winds give strength to the plants and crops, so the struggle to master the Torah makes the student grow.[213] According to Bullock, wisdom has charted a course that leads to Torah-centered Judaism.[214] In other words, Torah study leads to a life that honors God.

Moses knew the struggle it would be to know and follow the Law. He also must have understood the concept of learning to music. Today as the Jews study their weekly portions, they will sing at least the first *aliyah*. By the time the average Jewish boy becomes a teenager, he will have the entire Torah, not just Moses' song but the Five Books of Moses, committed to memory. Putting the Scripture to song is an effective way to remember the Word of God.

The Song of David

David also composed a song in his old age that is recorded in 2 Samuel 22:1–51. This Scripture forms the Haftarah portion that is read with ha'azinu. David's song echoed The Song of Moses as he expressed his gratitude to God for saving him from his enemies. David remembers where he has been, his struggles, and his pain. He recounts how the snares of death confronted him but that he turned to the Lord and called on Him for salvation. Then the God of heaven heard his cry, gave him strength, and scattered the enemy. David attributed his salvation to his pursuit of God's ways (21). David's pursuit of God's ways would have been an earnest study of the Torah.

---

[212] Ibid.

[213] Scherman, Rashi. *Chumash,* 2000, 1101.

[214] Hassell Bullock. JETS 52/1, March 2009. 15 *Wisdom, the "Amen" of Torah.* Franklin S. Dyrness, professor of biblical studies at Wheaton College, delivered this presidential address at the sixtieth annual meeting of the ETS in Providence, Rhode Island, on November 20, 2008.

Honoring the Torah

It is said that those who forget their history are doomed to repeat it, and with that in mind, Moses urged the people to remember their past in order to be informed and inspired by it. Blair notes that action in the present is conditioned by what one remembers of the past and that it produces compelling power.[215]

The Song of Moses is written to warn the people not to become apostate. In the last recorded words that Moses spoke to the people of Israel, Moses told them that the Torah was not an idle word for them; it was their life. The people were to honor the Torah at all times, in all generations. This is often obvious today in the way the Jew will reach out just to touch the very Word of God. Occasionally, in the old city of Jerusalem, one can see a giant Torah scroll being carried around the Western Wall Plaza as one celebrates one's bat mitzvah or bar mitzvah, a celebration of becoming an adult. There is usually much pomp and circumstance as one displays one's love of Torah.

There is a rabbinic parable told about two sisters. Both sisters were married but lived quite different lives. One was rich with many material possessions, and the other was poor. The rich sister could have anything she desired, yet she was very unhappy. The poor sister had one dress and hardly enough food to eat, yet she was very happy. The poor sister asked her rich sister, "Why are you so sad?" The rich sister answered, "My husband treats me disrespectfully, he embarrasses me in public, and he calls me stupid and useless. You, however, have everything. Your husband loves you, and he listens to you and encourages you. He values your opinion, and in public, he treats you with dignity. He treats you like a wife. My husband treats me worse than he treats the servants."

This parable is told to teach us the complaint of the Torah itself. Many well-to-do communities will dress up the Torah, parade it around the mall, and hang jewels on it to make impressive displays of tradition yet pay no attention to what the Torah actually says. The commandments are not taken seriously or incorporated into daily living. And there are poorer

---

[215] E. P. Blair. *An Appeal to Remembrance: The Memory Motif in Deuteronomy*, Int 15 (1961): 43. Quoted in J. G. McConville and J. G. Millar. *Time and Place in Deuteronomy*. Sheffield, England: Sheffield Academic Press, 1994, 46.

communities that cannot afford to dress up the Torah or their synagogue, yet they will hang on every word of the Torah. They fear the Lord and respect His Word. This is like the poor man who treated his wife respectfully.

Ironically, some Christian theologies will consider the Torah completely irrelevant to the New Testament believer. Yet the New Testament continually quotes the Torah as if it were relevant. Revelation 15:3 reiterates the Song of Moses.

> "And they sang the song of Moses, the bond-servant of God, and the song of the Lamb, saying, 'Great and marvelous are Your works, O Lord God, the Almighty; Righteous and true are Your ways, King of the nations!'"

For the New Testament believer, Jesus "was the Word, and the Word was with God, and the Word was God" (John 1:1). Jesus is the words of eternal life (John 6:6–8). Moses spoke to the Jew, the foreigner, and the stranger. May his teachings fall like rain upon all who read, for the Torah is not an idle for us, it is our life (Deuteronomy 32:47).

Yom Kippur

Yom Kippur (meaning "atonement") is a Jewish holiday that begins at sundown, 10 Tishrei on the Jewish calendar, and lasts twenty-five hours. Before the first Yom Kippur was celebrated, the children of Israel committed a grave sin. They knew it was prohibited to have any other gods before the one true God, yet they grew impatient for Moses to return from Mount Sinai so they pooled their resources (and their gold) and, with Aaron's help, they made a golden calf to worship. When Moses came down from the mountain, in his anger, he threw the tablets that contained the Ten Commandments. Despite his anger, Moses pleaded with God to forgive the people. After the month of Elul had passed, he ascended Mount Sinai again, and on Yom Kippur, atonement was achieved; Moses brought down the second set of tablets. Since then, it is believed by the Jew that every Yom Kippur wipes the slate clean, making atonement for their sin.[216]

---

[216] Karesh and Hurvitz. *Encyclopedia of Judaism*, 2006. Kindle location 1732.

Yom Kippur was the one day of the year that the high priest *(Kohen Gadol)* would enter the Holy of Holies. This was the inner court of the temple where the ark of the covenant was kept and the presence of God resided. Entrance into the Holy of Holies was forbidden any other day of the year, but this day was set aside to make special sacrifices to purify the temple and the people. To purify the temple, blood would be sprinkled around the sanctuary. To purify the people, blood would be put on a goat called the scapegoat, and it would be led outside the camp to be released into the wilderness.[217]

Since the temple was destroyed, Yom Kippur has been a day of self-denial. On the eve of Yom Kippur (Erev Yom Kippur), Jews gather in the synagogue before sundown to recite a prayer in Aramaic called the Kol Nidre ("All Vows"). The Jew believes this cancels all vows made between a person and God from this Yom Kippur to the next. Eating on Yom Kippur is strictly prohibited, so it is a special law to eat a big meal the afternoon before Yom Kippur begins. Apart from fasting, most will also refrain from bathing, wearing leather shoes, putting on perfumes or lotions, or engaging in marital relations. Many will also wear white, symbolizing purity.[218]

Yom Kippur is the most solemn day of the Jewish New Year as the Jews practice teshuva. The Jewish belief is that on Rosh Hashanah (ten days earlier on 1 Tishrei), the Book of Life and Death is opened and God will write the names of those who will be granted another year of life. For many, this decision is uncertain until Yom Kippur, when the final decision is sealed. Many fear for their lives and the lives of their loved ones. These ten days from Rosh Hashanah to Yom Kippur are known as "the Days of Awe." This is the reason the prayers of Yom Kippur are designed to inspire one to mend one's ways.[219]

During the last service of the day, there is an attitude of desperation as the ark (a cabinet where the Torah scrolls are kept) is left open and the

---

[217] Karesh and Hurvitz. *Encyclopedia of Judaism,* 2006. Kindle location 11876.

[218] Jewish Virtual Library. "Yom Kippur: History & Overview." https://www.jewish-virtuallibrary.org/jsource/Judaism/holiday4.html (accessed May 20, 2014).

[219] Rabbi Shraga Simmons. *ABC's of Yom Kippur.* http://www.aish.com/h/hh/yom-kippur/guide/ABCs-of-Yom-Kippur.html (accessed May 20, 2014).

congregation remains standing for the entire hour.[220] A prayer that is said on Rosh Hashanah and recited in all traditional synagogues is called "the great prayer," *U'Netaneh Tokef,* and it is attributed to Rabbi Amnon of Mainz. Included in this prayer is the following:

> On Rosh Hashanah will be inscribed and on Yom Kippur will be sealed … how many will pass from the earth and how many will be created; who will live and who will die … who will be impoverished and who will be enriched, who will be degraded and who will be exalted. But repentance, prayer, and charity remove the evil of the Decree![221]

Traditional Judaism teaches that every person can repent every day, but there are certain times of the year that are set aside specifically for that purpose; and the "gates of heaven" are more open to receive prayers. There are "gates of prayer" (our prayers open them) as well as gates that can be opened by tears and/or by prayers and words of children. In post-temple Judaism, it is therefore customary to wish others a "good final sealing" during the ten days of awe. Teshuva, tefillah (prayer), and tzedaka (charity) are three things many Christians could work harder at producing.

Yom Kippur is the pinnacle of the Jewish high holy days and has prophetic significance regarding the restoration of Israel, the second coming of Christ, and the final judgment of the world. It is also the day that reveals the high-priestly work of Jesus as our Kohen Gadol ("High Priest") after the order of Melchizedek (Hebrews 5:10, 6:20). Yom Kippur prophetically pictures the "Day of the Lord," also known as "the Day of Judgment." During the tribulation to follow the day of judgment, the New Testament insists that all of Israel will be saved, Jesus will physically return to Israel

---

[220] Tracey R Rich. *Judaism 101.* "Yom Kippur." http://www.jewfaq.org/holiday4. htm. (accessed May 20, 2014).

[221] My Jewish Learning. *U'Netaneh Tokef.* http://www.myjewishlearning.com/ holidays/Jewish_Holidays/Rosh_Hashanah/In_the_Community/Services/Prayers/ Mahzor_Content/Unetanah_Tokef.shtml?p=2 (accessed June 27, 2014).

to establish His kingdom on earth, and all the promises given to ethnic Israel through the prophets will be fulfilled.[222]

The New Testament teaches that Christians (messianic Jews included) have complete access to the throne of God and have a permanent "sealing" by the grace and love of God, given through the life and shed blood of Jesus (Ephesians 1:13, 4:30; 2 Corinthians 1:21–22). Leviticus 17:11 describes the sacrificial blood that was offered by the High Priest on the altar to make atonement for the souls of God's children. Because of Jesus, the believer has a High Priest of the New Covenant.

Attending a Yom Kippur service with a group of messianic Jews and Torah-observant Christians on Yom Kippur is remarkably different from that of the Orthodox Jewish synagogue in that it is a joyous celebration of freedom. They pray loudly and with passion. They sing, "These Are the Days of Elijah" with celebratory spirit. They bring their own shofars and blow them as a form of worship. When they read together from the Scripture, their gratitude for their eternal freedom is immense. It is not like a typical Christian gathering. That could be because they remember where they have been and how far they have come. For many Christians, the discovery of their need for a Savior and receiving salvation happen at the same time, meaning most do not know they need to be saved until they are. For the Jew growing up on the Torah, they believe that unless they pray enough, repent enough, and give enough, there is no hope for them. Therefore, when they hear that Jesus' shed blood on the cross at Golgotha permanently atoned for everyone's sins, including theirs, and they believe it, they can truly understand the magnitude of God's grace.

Sukkot

> You shall keep the Feast of Booths seven days, when you have gathered in the produce from your threshing floor and your winepress. You shall rejoice in your feast, you and your son and your daughter, your male servant and

---

[222] John Parsons. *Behold the Goat of God! Yeshua as Korban Ha'Olam*, Hebrew for Christians. http://www.hebrew4christians.com/Holidays/Fall_Holidays/Yom_Kippur/Goat_of_God/goat_of_god.html (accessed May 20, 2014).

your female servant, the Levite, the sojourner, the fatherless, and the widow who are within your towns. For seven days you shall keep the feast to the Lord your God at the place that the Lord will choose, because the Lord your God will bless you in all your produce and in all the work of your hands, so that you will be altogether joyful.

—Deuteronomy 16:13–15

Sukkot begins just after sundown on 15 Tishrei in the Jewish calendar. They celebrate the festival for seven days, during which time all are commanded to dwell in a Sukkah. As previously stated, Sukkot is also known as "the Feast of Tabernacles," "the Feast of Booths," and "the Festival of the Ingathering." The Feast of Tabernacles is a little misleading because *tabernacle* refers to the *mishkan* (temple), not the huts the Torah instructs one to live in for seven days.

We read about Sukkot in Leviticus 23:34 and Deuteronomy 16:13. This festival is characterized by the outdoor Sukkah huts and the four species of plants that are waved each day. Today everything needed to build the Sukkah as well as a complete set of the four species can be purchased from a reliable distributor or a local Jewish bookstore with a rabbinical seal certifying their validity. In biblical times, Sukkot was considered a very important holiday. Detailed readings of the laws regarding the *mo'adim,* or "appointed times," can be found in Leviticus 22–23, Numbers 29, and Deuteronomy 14–16.

Sukkot is a time of great joy celebrating confidence in having received a "good judgment" for the coming year. This joy comes from the comfort in believing their sins were forgiven on Yom Kippur for another year. It is a special commandment to rejoice on Sukkot. In the days of the kings, Sukkot was a time of such great joy that it was simply known as "the Feast" (1 Kings 12:32). Number 29 describes many sacrifices were made during these seven days.[223]

The book of Ecclesiastes is read on Shabbat during Sukkot. The theme of Ecclesiastes is the folly of worldly pleasures rather than more eternal spiritual pursuits. This is the time to renew fellowship with our Creator.

---

[223] Simmons. *ABC's of Sukkot,* 2014. http://www.aish.com/h/su/dits/62549892.html.

Some have a custom to stay up all night reading the book of Deuteronomy. There is no work on the first two days, so it is a time to invite friends and neighbors to the Sukkah to celebrate a new sense of freedom. "Some commentators take the term 'booths' literally, as the tents that sheltered Israel for forty years; others say that it refers figuratively to the miraculous *Clouds of Glory* that protected the nation during those years. Thus Sukkot is a time to rejoice in God's concern for the well-being of His children."[224]

Living in the Sukkah is a reminder that the Israelites lived in huts for forty years while they wandered the desert. It is also a good reminder that God is ultimately the one who protects, not the home itself, just as He protected the Israelites in the desert.

The Sukkah

The structure of the Sukkah is exceedingly detailed in the Mishna and Talmud.[225]

According to Rabbi Elozor Barclay and Rabbi Titzchok Jeager, construction should take place the day after Yom Kippur. Anyone, including women and children, can build a Sukkah, but the charge is that every man must build one. The first thing one is to do in building the Sukkah is to drive a nail into a block of wood. The Sukkah can be built anywhere but not under a roof or an overhanging balcony, not even under a tree. The roof *(s'chach)* must be made from material that grows from the ground. The Sukkah must be at least twenty-seven square inches and it must have at least two and a half walls. The walls can be of any material, as long as they are sturdy enough to withstand a normal wind. One can make the walls from the side of a building, a hedge, or bushes. It is acceptable for two or three walls to be a hedge. The roof must cover the Sukkah so that it gives more shade than sun during the daytime, yet it should be open enough so that the stars are visible through the roof at night. The roof material can only be added after the walls are in place.[226]

---

[224] Scherman. *Chumash,* 2000, 688.

[225] Israel W Slotki, Slotki. *Soncino Babylonian Talmud Sukkah.* Talmudic Books, Kindle ed. Teaneck, New Jersey: Talmudic Books, 2012. Kindle location 166.

[226] Simmons. *ABC's of Sukkot,* 2014. http://www.aish.com/h/su/dits/62549892.html.

The Sukkah is designated as "home" for the seven days of the festival, so it is customary to decorate the interior and exterior with fruits and flowers and Jewish paraphernalia. During meals, celebrants traditionally pay tribute to the seven great leaders of Israel (Abraham, Isaac, Jacob, Moses, Aaron, Joseph, and David). Each leader has a day set aside for him, and some even set an extra place at the table, much like the place set for Elijah at the Passover meal.

The Four Species

On Sukkot, it is law to wave the four species, or *arba minim* mentioned in Leviticus 23:40. These are made into a bouquet or centerpiece and waved before the Lord every day. The four species are *esrog* (choice fruit), *lulav* (palm fronds), *hadas* (thick branches), and *arava* (river willows). The Babylonian Talmud (Sukkah 31–34) refers to this bouquet as *hoshanot*. These are to be bound together—two willows on the left, one palm branch in the center, and three palms on the right—then lifted together with the esrog and shaken three times in all directions, as a symbol of God's mastery over all creation. The Four Species are waved each day in the synagogue, during the recitation of the Hallel prayers of praise (readings from Psalms 113 to 118). Hallel is followed by hoshanot, where everyone circles a Torah scroll held on the *bimah* (elevated place). Hoshanot is named because of the recurrent expression *hoshana* or *hoshi'aNa,* meaning "save, I pray!"[227]

Shmini Atzeret and Simchat Torah

Shmini Atzeret is a separate holiday immediately following Sukkot. Shmini Atzeret literally means the "Eighth Day of Assembly." At this time, the busy activity of Sukkot stops. It is a time to focus on the relationship with God as special prayers are recited in the synagogue, although the obligation to sit in the Sukkah no longer applies.[228]

Two days after Sukkot is Simchat Torah. This day is set aside to celebrate the completion of the Torah reading cycle as it begins again. In

---

[227] Ibid.
[228] Ibid.

the traditional synagogue, all the Torah scrolls are taken out of the ark and the congregation dances "seven circuits" with great joy and song. Although Simchat Torah and Shmini Atzeret are separate holidays, they are celebrated on the same day in Israel.[229] More on the *dance of the Torah* will be included in the next section.

Messianic Shadows

Many messianic believers adhere to the idea that Jesus was born on Sukkot. Though there is no proof, there seems to be less proof to substantiate a December birthday. When looking at the origin of the December 25 birthday, the first known reference to commemorating the birth of Jesus on this date was in AD 354. At that time, half the Roman Empire celebrated Jesus' birthday on January 6. December 25 was first chosen as Jesus' birthday to replace a pagan Roman holiday called Saturnalia. This was the winter solstice festival originally marking the end of the planting season in honor of Saturn, the god of sowing or seed, who represented agriculture and fertility. Public Saturnalia banquets were being held as early as 217 BC. The early church, in an attempt to get rid of the pagan holiday, declared the twenty-fifth day of December the official birthday of Jesus. This may have been changed for the sole purpose of control over the pagans, although Saturnalia continued to be celebrated even after Constantine legalized Christianity in AD 313. The twelve days that separate December 25 and January 6 is what the phrase *the Twelve Days of Christmas* refers to.[230]

Again, there is no proof that Jesus birthday is on Sukkot, as all evidence is circumstantial; however, there are some compelling arguments. First, we know Jesus was thirty years old when he started his ministry (Luke 3:23). Most scholars agree his ministry lasted three and a half years until his death on the cross in the month of Nisan, six months earlier than Tishrei. We read in the Gospels that there was a census taken (Luke 2:1), and those in power would most likely have used an opportunity like Sukkot to have the census. Joseph and Mary were coming from Nazareth

---

[229] Simmons. *ABC's of Sukkot*, 2014. http://www.aish.com/h/su/dits/62549892.html.
[230] Elesha Coffman. *Christian History*. "Why December 25?" http://www.christianitytoday.com/ch/news/2000/dec08.html (accessed May 29, 2014).

(Luke 2:4) and would likely come for the census at the same time as they made the pilgrimage home for one of the three festivals or mo'edim (appointed times). In our day, most people would not fly halfway across our country to be counted. One would likely tie that into a trip home for Thanksgiving, Christmas, or perhaps an annual family reunion on the Fourth of July. We know Mary and Joseph were very religious, and it is plausible they made that trip three times a year for Passover, Shavu'ot, and Sukkot (Shalosh Regalim), as the commandment states in Exodus 23:14.

We know that the shepherds were out in their fields tending to their sheep when the angels came to tell them of the news of the Messiah's birth (Luke 2:10) and that shepherds would not likely be out in the field in the middle of winter.

Sukkot is known as the Festival of Joy, so as the angels greeted the shepherds, they would have been using this Sukkot greeting: "I bring you good news of great joy that will be for all the people." In America, if someone said, "Joy to the world," our first thought would be Christmas. At the time Luke wrote his gospel, the Jews' first thought would have been Sukkot.

Digging a little deeper, we can find that an angel of the Lord spoke to Zacharias and told him that his wife would become pregnant and have a son like Elijah who would prepare the way for the Lord (Luke 1:13–17). Traditionally, it is believed that one like Elijah would come at Passover. Even today, it is customary for the Jew to set a place at the table for Elijah on Passover, so it is reasonable to think that John was born on Nissan 15. Luke 1:36 tells us that the angel Gabriel visited Mary in Elizabeth's sixth month of pregnancy, thus John the Baptist would be six months older than Jesus. If that were true, it would put Jesus' birthday at 15 Tishrei, the first day of Sukkot. One more compelling thought is that if it were true that His birthday was the first day of Sukkot, then He would have been eight days old on Shmini Atzeret, the eighth day of the assembly, the same day He would have been circumcised. This day, like the first day, is a day of sacred assembly when the Jews complete the Torah reading cycle and start over in Bereshit (Genesis). The following day is Simchat Torah, considered to be a time of fulfillment. Again, there is no proof in the Scriptures as to when Yeshua's birthday is. This is all circumstantial evidence but not without merit.

The word Torah (הרות) is a function word that articulates our responsibility. Leviticus 23:41 says, "You shall rejoice before the Lord your God seven days. You shall celebrate it as a feast to the Lord for seven days in the year. It is a statute forever throughout your generations." The New American Standard Bible translation pronounces, "It shall be a perpetual statute throughout your generations." Zechariah 14:16 declares, "Then it will come about that any who are left of all the nations that went against Jerusalem will go up from year to year to worship the King, the Lord of hosts, and to celebrate the Feast of Booths." Why is this the only holiday mentioned here? Could it be that this will one day be an international birthday party of Jesus? Okay, even if the arguments for a Sukkot birthday for Jesus are not convincing, Sukkot is one of the three mo'edim, where the commandment is to gather and give thanks. It has been clearly commanded that Sukkot "be a perpetual statute forever throughout all your generations." Deuteronomy 16 specifically states it is applicable to even the sojourner, making it seem irresponsible for the Gentile, the sojourner, to be ambivalent or complacent about this festival. Answer the question "Why does the Jew celebrate Sukkot and the Christian does not?" Galatians 3:24 explains.

> Therefore, the Law has become our tutor to lead us to Christ, so that we may be justified by faith. But now that faith has come, we are no longer under a tutor. For you are all sons of God through faith in Christ Jesus. For all of you who were baptized into Christ have clothed yourselves with Christ. There is neither Jew nor Greek, there is neither slave nor free man, there is neither male nor female; for you are all one in Christ Jesus. And if you belong to Christ, then you are Abraham's descendants, heirs according to promise.

Sukkot is an appointed time to celebrate the harvest and salvation. Building the Sukkah starts the day after Yom Kippur, and it is to be started by driving a nail into a block of wood. This is a reminder of the image of the nails being driven into the hands of Jesus. He was crucified, buried, and rose from the grave so the Spirit of the living God could dwell within the believer.

In the New Testament, there is no evidence that the Christian is obligated to keep any biblical festival and certainly no obligation to observe any human made or nonbiblical ritual like building a Sukkah hut. Romans 6:14 exclaims we are not under the law of Moses but under grace.[231] While the Christian is not obligated, he or she is free to celebrate any holidays if he or she desires to do so. It is allowed by God, but not always edifying (1 Corinthians 10:23). Some Christians celebrate Christmas, and others do not. Jesus rebuked the sages for making their traditions more important than the Word of God to the point that the Word of God was of no effect (Mark 7:8, 9, 13). Another reason not to observe the festivals is if we expect any spiritual benefit from them other than pointing to Christ. Some celebrate the festivals as a way to flaunt their rich heritage or even their knowledge of the Old Testament culture. Yet the Scripture explains that when people accept Jesus as their personal Savior, they receive a new identity. Galatians 3:28 says that whatever a person's background, Jew or Gentile, slave or free, man or woman, none of it matters anymore. The Christian is free in Christ, and if he or she is holding onto some cultural heritage thinking it will give them a better standing with God, they are really missing the point Jesus tried so hard to convey. Culture cannot replace Christ. Relying on these traditions for social status might be a sign that one is weak in the faith (Romans 14:1), and relying on anything other than Jesus' death on the cross for salvation would obviously be indicative of no faith. The old traditions can serve, however, as lessons in one's walk of faith. Therefore, we must not judge those who observe traditions differently (Colossians 2:16), for all will stand before God and give an account, their own account (Romans 14:3–6, 10). We must strive to relate to and not offend, those with whom we disagree (1 Corinthians 10:32) without compromising our personal convictions. As Paul argued, "Let every man be persuaded in his own mind" (Romans 14:5).

---

[231] Bruce Scott. *The Feasts of Israel: Seasons of the Messiah.* Bellmawr, New Jersey: The Friends of Israel Gospel Ministry, 1997, 181.

133

CHAPTER 12

This Is the Blessing

"Vezot Ha'berachah"
Deuteronomy 33:1–34:12

Vezot ha'Berachah is the last portion of the Torah cycle. This Hebrew word means "this is the blessing." This parsha is read on Simchat Torah, two days after Sukkot. Tradition says when one begins to study Torah, the Devil says, "Though they have begun to study it, they will not finish it." When one finishes the cycle on Simchat Torah, the Devil will make another accusation, saying, "Though they have finished it, they will not study it again."[232] To the glory of God, the Jew will begin Genesis the same day the last parsha is read in Deuteronomy. This day is set aside to celebrate the completion of the Torah reading cycle and the beginning of the new to imply that while the end of the Torah has been reached, one should never be finished reading the Torah. This shows the eternality of God's Word. In some synagogues, the Torah scroll is unrolled and wrapped around the congregation during Simchat Torah service, and everyone gets a chance to *dance* with the Torah. The Jews' love for the Word of God is far more passionate than most Christians'. It is not uncommon to see the people in Israel reach out to touch a Torah scroll with their fingers and then bring their fingers to their lips as if to taste the sweetness of His Word. Scripture is kept in the phylacteries worn by the men during their morning prayers.

---

[232] Boaz Michael. *Simchat Torah.* First Fruits of Zion. http://ffoz.org/resources/edrash/vezot_habracha/simchat_torah.php (accessed May 20, 2014).

The mezuzah hangs on the doorposts, the gates of their homes, and even hotel rooms containing Shema. Again, the Jew will touch the mezuzah when entering and exiting a room.

This last portion contains Moses' final words to the Israelites. Before Moses ascended Mount Nebo to die, he blessed those who had followed him through the desert for forty years (Deuteronomy 33:1). Moses blessed each of the tribes, although not in their birth order. With the exception of Simeon, all were blessed.

Much is written that when Moses learned his hour of death was near, he cried out to God, "Wait until I have blessed Israel. All my life long they had no pleasant experiences with me, for I constantly rebuked them and admonished them to fear God and fulfill the commandments, therefore do I not wish to depart out of this world before I have blessed them."[233]

Moses loved the people of Israel even though he could have blamed them for his wanderings. Midrash tells us Moses appealed to God to let him enter the Promised Land but God refused because of six sins that he committed. The first sin Moses committed was refusing to go to Pharaoh and demand he set God's people free (Exodus 4:13). The second sin is found in Exodus 5:23 where Moses accused God of willfully making conditions bad for the Israelites. Twice Moses tested God during Korach's rebellion (Numbers 16:29–30), and he slandered the people on two other occasions (Numbers 20:10, 32:14). Scripture clearly states that because of the incident at Meribah (Numbers 20:10), Moses and Aaron would not bring the people into the land given to them. At first glance, we see God tell Moses to speak to the rock, and in turn, Moses has a bad attitude and strikes the rock, not just once but twice. Moses trusted God with his future but not enough to honor Him as holy in front of the people. According to some, the bottom line was not his attitude; it was not even his unbelief. Rather, it was his display of that unbelief in front of the people he was chosen to lead. According to the sages, that is what kept him out of the Promised Land.

---

[233] Ginzberg. *Legends,* 2010. Kindle location 13843.

The Blessing

It is not known with certainty who wrote the last chapters, including Moses' blessing, or if it was later appended to the book of Deuteronomy. Two possibilities exist. One possibility is that Joshua wrote the remaining verses, or as Rashi comments, "The Holy One, Blessed is He, dictated these words to Moses, and he wrote them with tears, rather than ink."[234] Rabbi Meir says, "Scripture itself says Moses wrote down this Torah and gave it to the priests" (Deuteronomy 31:9). He questions, "Is it possible that Moses gave the Torah while it was lacking even one letter?"[235]

Moses' last words are of blessing and reassurance—for ultimately Israel will fulfill its promise and be showered with divine rewards that will eclipse by far the horrors it has endured."[236] Moses' blessing begins with a poetic metaphor recalling the experience at Sinai. Moses continues declaring that God's Word was given because of His great love for them, "for they planted themselves at Your feet, bearing the yoke of Your utterances." Verse 4 says, "The Torah that Moses commanded us is the heritage of the congregation of Jacob" (Deuteronomy 33:3, 4).

According to Ramban, "The Torah is the heritage, not merely of those born of Jewish parents, but it is shared by every soul that joins the Jewish nation and accepts the Torah."[237] The sages say the word translated as "heritage" can also be translated as "married," meaning that the Jewish people and the Torah could be considered like bride and groom.[238]

Rabbi Mordechai Gifter explains that a heritage is the property of the heirs to preserve intact for all future generations.[239] The implication here is that the Torah would become an inheritance for all who would congregate with Jacob, including all who are "grafted in" (John 10:16, Romans 11:16–24).

There is plenty of debate among the scholars as to why Moses blessed the tribes in the order he did and why the tribe of Simeon is missing. One

---

[234] Scherman, Rashi. *Chumash*, 2000, 1122.

[235] Hammer. *The Classic Midrash*, 1995, 389.

[236] Scherman. *Chumash*, 2000, 1121.

[237] Scherman, Ramban. *Chumash*, 2000, 1113.

[238] Freedman. *Pesahim 49b*, 2012. Kindle location 7214.

[239] Scherman, Rabbi Mordechai Gifter. *Chumash*, 2000, 1113.

common thought on the exclusion of Simeon is his involvement with the slaughter at Shechem and his failure to repent after the incident of the golden calf.[240] Jacob did not bless the sons of Israel according to their birth order either (Genesis 49:1–28). It is interesting that Moses would be so determined to bless the people before he died. One could argue that it was the grumbling of the people that caused Moses to sin, therefore making them responsible for his loss. Still, it was Moses' final request to give a blessing to each of the tribes that could not be retracted (Genesis 27).

Moses' Death

After Moses blessed the people, God Himself buried him in the valley in the land of Moab, opposite Beth-Peor in an unknown place. To this day, his grave has not been found.

"Moses was 120 years old when he died. His eye was undimmed, and his vigor unabated, and the people of Israel wept for Moses in the plains of Moab thirty days" (Deuteronomy 34:7–8). There is a midrash stating that God kissed Moses at the moment of his death. This comes from the word *al-pi Adonai,* which can be translated "by the mouth of the Eternal."[241]

When Moses was alive, he was called "a man of God" (33:1), but when he died, he was called a "servant of God." Rabbi Bachya notes that this alludes to a higher status, as a servant is allowed to enter the inner chambers of the king whom he serves.

The Commissioning of Joshua

The commissioning of Joshua as new leader is the Haftarah for Vezot HaBerachah. God instructs Joshua to "be strong and of good courage" (chazak ve'ematz) three times (Deuteronomy 1:6, 7, 9). The Lord ended with these words: "Have I not commanded you? Be strong and courageous. Do not be frightened, and do not be dismayed, for the Lord your God is

---

[240] John Parsons. *Every Letter of Torah: Further Thoughts on Parashat Haberakhah.* http://www.hebrew4christians.com/Scripture/Parashah/Summaries/Vzot-Haberakhah/Letter/letter.html (accessed June 20, 2014).

[241] Scherman, Rashi. *Chumash,* 2000, 1122.

with you wherever you go" (Joshua 1:8–9). God tells Joshua three times to be strong and courageous, as if He knows being committed to the Torah takes deliberate action. God knew there would be times when it seemed easier to run to an idol or to a town like Nineveh (Jonah 2) than it would be to follow the Torah. One should note this is not a request God is making. This is a command followed by the reassurance that God would be with him wherever he went.

The New Jerusalem

Revelation 22:1–5 is a vision of the ultimate Promised Land. It is a glimpse of the New Jerusalem and the river that will flow from the throne of God down the streets of gold. One can almost taste the fruit and feel the warmth of the light that comes from all around. It is the new beginning, looking forward to the beginning of the Torah reading cycle again. It is not the end, but a new beginning.

The Dance of the Torah

The idea that the study of the Torah never ends is expressed in the joyous dance called *hakkofot*. This parsha, Vezot haBrachah, is customarily read on Simchat Torah ("Rejoicing of the Torah"). It is a day of rejoicing. The celebration that accompanies the Simchat Torah is traditionally done on the eighth day (Shmini Atzeret) after Sukkot. It is said that it is the Torah that needs to rejoice, but since it has no legs to dance, the congregation becomes the arms and legs of the Torah. In the synagogue, it is tradition to take the Torah in one's arms and dance around the aisles. This is the rejoicing of the Torah.

Messianic Judaism has developed the Davidic dance. It is possible it comes from a traditional folk dance that originally came from Romania called Horah.[242] While the most Orthodox of messianic Jewish congregations do not participate in this dance, in the more liberal congregations, it is common to find some in circles and dancing a very beautiful, slow,

---

[242] Bridger. *The New Jewish Encyclopedia*, sv "Horah," 1976, 210.

and graceful choreographed dance during the music.[243] This looks a little like an old folk dance but is very slow and graceful. Even in the Orthodox Jewish synagogue, where dancing is highly unusual, there is dancing on Simchat Torah.

Dance was a natural expression of worship in Israel. We can find it encouraged in Psalm 149:3. "Let them praise His name with dancing; Let them sing praises to Him with timbrel and lyre." Psalms 150:4 continues. "Praise Him with timbrel and dancing; Praise Him with stringed instruments and pipe."

The dance is rooted in the Song of the Sea. After Moses finished singing, Miriam "took a timbrel in her hand, and all the women followed her, with timbrels and dancing" (Exodus 15:20). Jeremiah tells us that when Messiah comes, there will be dancing (Jeremiah 31:13). When King David returned from battle with the Philistines, the women of Israel came out singing and dancing. When he brought the ark of the covenant back into Jerusalem, David himself danced.

In Hebrew, HaShem means "the name." It is how the reverent Jew refers to God, as you will not typically hear Orthodox Jewish men or women speak the name of God, and you certainly would not see them write it. I once asked an Orthodox Jewish woman how to pronounce YHWH, to which she replied, "We don't know, as we don't speak it out loud." To experience the reverence and constant repentance in her actions, words, and deeds is convicting, as our human propensity is to wander and become complacent.

Like the Jews in Moses' day, the Christian can learn to love the Word of God—living it, breathing it in and out, dancing with it, interacting with it, and proclaiming it. Orchos Chayim declares, "Make it your habit to fall asleep whilst learning Torah." The point is to tire yourself on Torah.[244] Let the Torah consume every shadow of life. The prophet Micah penned the words "Do justly, love mercy and walk humbly with your God" (6:8). All this implies action. While it is good to know the difference between right

---

[243] Boaz Michael Messianic and Davic Dance. http://ffoz.org/resources/edrash/beshalach/messianic_and_davidic_dance.php (accessed May 20, 2014).

[244] Reuven Brauner. *An Adaption of the Rosh's Sefer Orchos Chayim: The Pathways of Life.* Raanana, Israel: Talmudic Books, 2012, 6.

and wrong, Micah insists one is to "do" the right thing. To know what mercy is and to "love" mercy are not the same thing.

There is an old parable of a king who hired two workers to fill up a pit. The first one took one look at the size of the pit and said, "I will never be able to fill this pit!" Then he quit. The second worker said, "It does not matter if I ever finish. I am paid by the hour so this is job security for me!" The Talmud says, "Greater is the study of Torah than the rebuilding of the temple."[245] A person should never withhold himself from the words of the Torah even at the hour of death.[246] When the thought of reading through the Bible seems overwhelming, look to the Torah cycle. This allows one to do as much as possible without as much potential for failure. The end point of one's journey will be redemption without exile and a completeness of spirituality that needs no new excursions.[247] The Torah was put in charge to lead us to Messiah (Galatians 3:24). Jesus is the goal of the Torah. He is not the ending; rather, He is the beginning. "Do not think I have come to abolish the Torah ..." (Matthew 5:17).

The Final Message

Moses' final message is a warning to the Israelites of what they must endure. The final message of the New Testament also warns us of the same. "The Revelation of Jesus Christ, which God gave Him to show to His bond-servants, the things which must soon take place; and He sent and communicated it by His angel to His bond-servant John, who testified to the Word of God and to the testimony of Jesus Christ, even to all that he saw. Blessed is he who reads and those who hear the words of the prophecy, and heed the things which are written in it; for the time is near" (Revelation 1:1–3). Although the time and place are unknown, He who is the eternal Word and the goal of the Torah, the first and the last, the Alpha and Omega, the Alf and the Tav, speaks His final words. "'Yes, I am coming quickly.' Amen." (Revelation 22:20).

---

[245] Simon and Segal. *Megillah and Shekalim.* 16b, 2012. Kindle location 2917.

[246] Cohen. *Everyman's Talmud,* 1996, 136: Freedman. *Shabbath* 83b, 2012. Kindle location 16069.

[247] Schneerson and Sacks. *A Parsha Anthology,* 2000, 288.

I have repeatedly witnessed in Israel the Jew who sees the Torah and reaches out to touch it as if to touch the tzitzit of God himself. According to R' Yehudah Halevi, the Torah itself is the king, for it is Israel's ultimate authority. When Scripture laments there was no king in Israel (Judges 18:1), it means that the people lagged in their obedience to the Torah. Indeed, for one to say that he believes in God but not in his Torah is the same as denying God Himself, for a king without authority is not a king.[248]

There is a great lesson to learn from Simchat Torah. You see, one cannot find the Torah applicable until one commits to the study of the Torah. There can be no love for the Torah without finding its applicability to the lives of the living and their current individual circumstances. When that love for Torah is found, freedom will prevail. And it all starts with deliberate study of the Torah.

The love for Scripture I have witnessed while visiting the Holy Land has inspired me to pray that I will never finish studying the Torah. In the conclusion of the book of Deuteronomy, it is customary to proclaim, "Chazak! Chazak! Venischazeik! Be strong! Be strong! And may we be strengthened!" This is followed immediately by Genesis 1:1, which says, "In the beginning God created the heavens and the earth ..."

---

[248] Scherman. Yehudah. *Chumash*, 2000, 1114.

CHAPTER 13

Conclusion

Many years ago, I noticed that a vast number of people are disheartened by their circumstances. Then I asked myself, "What discourages these people?" As I searched for that answer, I had to notice the infinite number of reasons to feel "not good enough." Is this an issue of pride, or simply the universal longing to make a difference? What I found was that everything can be discouraging, and anything can imprison one's joy, but at the root, it is the same: an unrelenting desire for freedom. It seems to be the one thing that everyone wants, and not many seem to find. "For the gate is small and the way is narrow that leads to life" (Matthew 7:14). Sydney Smith once said, "A great deal of talent is lost to the world for want of a little courage. Every day sends to their graves obscure men whose timidity prevented them from making a first effort."[249] Discouragement can be crippling. Many of the problems experienced today and the daily battles with discouragement stem from a lack of clarity about what truth and freedom really are.

This is the era of the selfie, the iPhone, and the iPad. It is the era of instant results, fast food, and a fast-paced lifestyle, while overstimulated families become trapped in a prison of wanting more. When an opportunity comes along, be it a new job, a new ministry, or a new home, the response is often like the shark in a feeding frenzy. Many do not take time to consult God until after decisions have been made and regret is one's

---

[249] Sydney Smith. "Brainy Quote" (accessed May 20, 2014). http://www.brainyquote.com/quotes/quotes/s/sydneysmit100934.html.

mantra. This is the lifestyle of self-fulfillment and self-preservation. When clarity about truth is absent or dimmed, poor choices will be made and feeding frenzies are bound to happen.

A self-centered mind-set will go in search of freedom and happiness because it is what they want. When pride is at the root, it is only a matter of time before one begins to worry about achieving this freedom and happiness. Ultimately, this will turn into anger, bitterness, impure thoughts, and wrong actions. This then creates guilt, which turns to boredom and gives a lack of purpose to the point one becomes dependent and a slave to self. On the other hand, when we live a humble life, focused on God and His kingdom, we will become a slave to Christ, being a servant of God and yielding to His call. This will bring pure thoughts, rights actions, and a clear conscience. We will find ourselves with a spiritual hunger and purpose, with conviction, independence, and inner joy. Without the strife, freedom and happiness will be the result.

The solution then lies in the quest for truth. Many have no problem reading history books about World War I or the Battle of Gettysburg, believing every detail the author pens as gospel truth. Why, then, is it so hard for those same people to read the Scripture and accept it as truth? Many people delight in spending a rainy Saturday curled up in front of a fireplace while reading for ten hours yet never think of reading the Scripture for more than ten minutes at a time. Many spend a lifetime searching for good biographies to read, yet it never occurs to them to read God's biography.

I have found that a deep study of the Torah can unfold much meaning, bringing great understanding to the words of Jesus. "The written testimony (God's biography) is enshrined in both Testaments, and both remain indispensable."[250] It is obvious that in the church, there are many different theologies in play. According to Dr. John Mayer, in Minneapolis alone there are over 3,569 churches from 241 different denominations or religions.[251] This is the epitome of struggle with truth. I see a pendulum that has swung from the far right to the far left as many interpret Scriptures of the New Testament with total disregard for the text of the Old Testament.

---

[250] F. F. Bruce. *The Cannon of Scripture.* Downers Grove: InterVarsity Press, 1988, 275.
[251] John Mayer. *Church History: Cityview Report.* Interviewed by Donna Stundahl, Maple Plain, Minnesota, June 1, 2014.

For many, "church" is built on emotion, and when times get tough, faith is lost. Others see emotion as sin and gasp if the pastor makes a joke on the pulpit. People can work for their salvation through ministries and service or they can be bent on proving it is by grace they are saved. Could it be that the truth is where the pendulum stops swinging? Could there ever be unity in the body of Christ? "Behold, how good and how pleasant it is for brothers to dwell in unity!" (Psalm 133:1). Paul pleaded, "I, the prisoner of the Lord, implore you to walk in a manner worthy of the calling with which you have been called" (Ephesians 4:1), being diligent to preserve the unity of the Spirit in the bond of peace (4:3).

Chinitz points out the unity of the Torah being applied to all peoples equally in Exodus 12:49. "The same Law shall apply to the native as to the stranger who sojourns among you."[252] Paul concurred with Moses, explaining that all Scripture is inspired and relevant and useful for teaching, training, and rebuking (2 Timothy 3:16). Coupled with 1 Corinthians 14:21, Torah would then be synonymous with Old Testament and New Testament Scriptures. Torah is the entire Word inspired by God himself. Jesus said, "If you love me you will obey my commands."

Historical Interaction

Paul looked to history, the roots of Judaism, as he searched for the meaning of the story he believed climaxed with Jesus Christ. History is where the Christian needs to go if one is to understand the applicability and unity of the entire text. Wright declares, "For too long we have read Scripture with nineteenth-century eyes and sixteenth-century questions. It's time to get back to reading with first-century eyes and twenty-first-century questions."[253]

Those who keep the Torah say, "Keep the Torah for the sake of Torah." This implies that one should not keep the Torah for the rewards but as an act of obedience. Boaz Michael sees another reason for keeping the Torah: as a matter of discipleship. Emphasis on becoming a disciple of Jesus rather

---

[252] Chinitz. *The Word Torah in the Torah*, 2005.

[253] N. T. Wright. *Justification: God's Plan & Paul's Vision*, Kindle ed. Downers Grove, InterVarsity Press Academic, 2009. Kindle location 363

than being Torah observant needs to be the focus.[254] Campenhausen would agree, stating, "Even an Old Testament read with critical eyes is still the book of a history which leads to Christ and indeed points toward Him, and without Him cannot be understood."[255]

Phil Goble agreed with the apostle Paul and argued that the root of Christianity is a transcultural Judaism.[256] However, translators do not always know the principles of cross-cultural interpretation and at times have required converts to abandon their culture completely.[257] There have been times (in recent years) where messianic Jews were required to prove their Christianity by eating a ham sandwich.[258] Yet the Scripture is clear in Colossians 2:16–17. "Therefore no one is to act as your judge in regard to food or drink in respect to festival or a new moon or a Sabbath day—things which are a mere shadow of what is to come; but the substance belongs to Christ."

It seems strange that the gospel would need to be contextualized to witness to a Jew when the root of Christianity is Jewish, Jesus Himself was Jewish, and the gospel is Jewish. The only reason one would need to contextualize the gospel for the Jew would be that the gospel has fallen so far away from what it was intended to be that the Jew would not recognize it. That begs the question "Would Jesus?"

In the first century, when children turned six years of age, it was the responsibility of adults to "stuff them like an ox" with Torah study. A few of the most outstanding Bet Midrash students were compelled to seek out a famous rabbi to study under. This would entail leaving their friends and family for years. These students were called *talmidim* in Hebrew, which is translated to "disciple." However, being a good American student is not much like being a good talmid. For the former, there is more desire

---

[254] Boaz Michael. First Fruits of Zion. https://ffoz.com/about-our-company.html (accessed June 9, 2014).

[255] Hans von Campenhausen. *The Formation of the Christian Bible.* London: Augsburg Fortress Publishing, 1972, 333

[256] David H. Stern, PhD. *Restoring the Jewishness of the Gospel: A Message for Christians Condensed from Messianic Judaism,* Kindle ed. Clarksville: Lederer Books, 2009. Kindle location 204.

[257] Stern. *Restoring the Jewishness,* 2009. Kindle location 207.

[258] Ibid. Kindle location, 234.

to get good grades and reach the completion of education; a talmid or talmida wants to be like the teacher.[259] This relationship involved walking together, sitting together, and eating together. If the rabbi prayed, the student prayed. If the rabbi crossed his leg, the student crossed his leg. The talmidim mimicked the rabbi's every move until eventually they would have the lifestyle of their rabbi and then go on to teach other talmidim.

Jesus summoned the twelve whom He wanted so that "they would be with Him and that He could send them out to preach" (Mark 3:13–19). Jesus explained that once a pupil was fully trained, he would be like his teacher (Luke 6:40)—not above him or below him but following the example he set (John 13:15). This implies that the present day talmid of Jesus must be no less focused on the rabbi Jesus. The Christian should be with Jesus in His Word and following Him even when unsure of the final destination.[260] This would include learning the historical context, cultural propensities, and literary traditions of the day. Language should also be studied to understand idioms that may be implied as well.

Study of the text should be thorough. James told the new believers in Jesus Christ to look intently into the perfect Law of liberty (James 1:25). In this passage, we do not see the implication of the word translated as "looketh" until we looketh deeper into the language. Most people who read their Bibles would say they "looketh into the Bible." However, the Greek word used in this text is *parakoopto*. It means to bend beside, stoop down, and lean over so as to peer within. Parakoopto is more than reading the Scripture. It would be like looking for a diamond that fell out of your wedding ring onto the floor. It is searching for something known to have much value to you personally. One would find himself stooped down, on hands and knees, searching the floor. Parakoopto implies not giving up until you find it.

Stern insists that the Jewishness of the gospel be restored, claiming, "Restoring the Jewishness of the gospel means filling out the content of

---

[259] Keri Wyatt Kent. *Deeper into the Word: New Testament.* "A Disciple of Rabbi Jesus: Exploring the Meaning of Disciple." http://www.smallgroups.com/articles/2012/disciplerabbijesus.html (accessed May 20, 2014).

[260] Ray Vander Laan, That the World May Know Ministries. *The Rabbi and His Talmidim* (2003) http://followtherabbi.com/guide/detail/rabbi-and-talmidim.pdf (accessed May 20, 2014).

the gospel in all its fullness as it pertains to Jews and to the relationship between the Jewish people and the church."[261] This would include the entire counsel of God. The meaning of Scripture does not change and cannot mean something it never meant from the start; it is only its applicability that changes. If one does not understand what the author meant in the first place, how could one grasp its full meaning?

Research has shown throughout this exploration that Jesus and His disciples reiterated these concepts so highly valued by the Jewish community. Concepts, such as lashon hara and arevut, were well-known and had much value in their lives and their teaching.

Sterns argues that Paul's church was the messianic congregation, but after Christianity became the state religion of Rome in the early fourth century, much of the church body consisted of Gentiles who did not believe in the work of Jesus as Messiah. Soon enough, it became impossible for the Jew to express publicly both Jewishness and belief in Jesus. To become Christian meant to leave the Jewish community and renounce any Jewish traditions.[262] However, Jesus made it clear that He did not come to abolish the Law (Matthew 5:17).

We need to start by making every effort to understand the text of the New Testament as its first century hearers would have understood it. From there, we can understand how it applies to our situations in life. Though we are not expected to apply the gospel in the same way it was applied in the first century, we must understand Scripture properly before we can apply it to our own circumstances in the appropriate way. Stern does not describe a new philosophy. He expresses a familiar approach, which normally leads to asking whether a given New Testament command is to be applied literally or understood as a general principle behind the written command. For example, in reference to 1 Corinthians 11:2–16, must a woman today cover her head in a congregation meeting? Or was this requirement related only to the first-century life situation, so that the modern application is to dress modestly by current standards?[263] Should the congregations in America be greeting each other with a holy kiss on the lips as they did in the first

---

[261] Stern. *Restoring the Jewishness of the Gospel,* 2009. Kindle location 328.

[262] Stern. *Restoring the Jewishness of the Gospel,* 2009. Kindle location 433.

[263] Ibid., 337.

century? Or is it the principle that is important: to greet others with sincerity and friendship? To know the culture when the text was written will bring one closer to the author's intended meaning. Ryrie argues that everyone seeking to find application, such as by "turning the other cheek" to life in the twenty-first century, has to make some adjustments to a strict, literal interpretation of Scripture.[264]

First Timothy 4:13 reminds the believer to give attention to the public reading of Scripture. Does that imply reading two or three verses each week from the New Testament? I surmise Jesus and the disciples would have understood that as reading through the Torah in its entirety every year. Most Christians today have never read the entire Torah, much less during public gatherings year after year. Some Christians today treat the Scriptures with more reverence as they stand for the reading, yet it is still only a few verses, during which time it is not uncommon to hear the chatter of someone annoyed by the fact that the pastor has asked them to stand.

It is the custom of the Jews to pray before the Scripture is read, saying, "Blessed art thou Lord our God, King of the universe, who sanctifies us with Thy commandments and commands us to engross ourselves in the words of Torah." It is worth noting that the word translated as engross (la'asok) means to engage, or to immerse oneself. La'asok comes from the Hebrew root "busy," implying that all should be busy with the study of the Torah.[265] Jesus said, "If you continue in my word, you will know the truth and the truth will set you free" (John 8:31b–32). Finding the truth takes continued, deliberate study. The Talmud says, "Only he is free who is committed to Torah"[266] (Avoth 6:2).

What then, is the problem in Christianity today? Has the Word become too much of a burden? Has it become less applicable than it was in the first century? On the other hand, has freedom become a concept misunderstood as independence or autonomy? Throughout this exploration, we have seen the same concepts laid out in the Torah and then repeated

[264] Ryrie. *Dispensationalism Today,* 1969, 106–108.

[265] John Parsons. *La'asok be'divrei Torah: Customary Blessing before Torah Study.* http://www.hebrew4christians.net/Blessings/Daily_Blessings/Torah_Study/torah_study.html (accessed May 20, 2014).

[266] Israelstam, Segal, and Lazarus. *Makkoth, Eduyyoth, and Aboth,* 2012. Kindle location 8363.

by Jesus and His disciples. It is apparent that Jesus emphasized the same concepts, which were more important in Moses' day. Jesus found the applicability and reiterated it as a command to His followers, calling it freedom.

Freedom is a gift from God in Christ for all who are willing to receive it. It is a major theme running throughout the Old Testament and New Testament. In Moses' day, God freed the people from Egypt. In David's day, God freed them from the Philistines. Two thousand years ago, God made a way to free all of humankind—not just the Jew but the Gentile as well. Paul argued, "There is neither Jew nor Greek, there is neither slave nor free man, there is neither male nor female: for you are all one in Christ Jesus" (Galatians 3:28). God still leads His followers out of captivity to a land full of promise and freedom.

As the end times draw near, it is more important than ever before to read the text inspired by God, the Old Testament and New Testament, over and over again. Freedom is not easy and is often equally ambiguous, but truth tells us that if we seek, we shall find the freedom that everyone so desperately pursues. True freedom is knowing that Jesus Christ died for all who choose to experience the eternal freedom of heaven.

APPENDIX A

Torah Portions

Name of Portion	Verses	Haftarah Portion
Genesis		
B'reisheet	1:1–6:8	Isa. 42:5–43:11 (42:5–21)
Noach	6:9–11:32	Isa. 54:1–55:5 (54:1–10)
Lech Lecha	12:1–17:27	Isa. 40:27–41:16
Vayera	18:1–22:24	2 Kings 4:1–37 (4:1–23)
Chayei Sarah	23:1–25:18	1 Kings 1:1–31
Toldot	25:19–28:9	Mal. 1:1–2:7
Vayetze	28:10–32:3	Hos. 12:13–14:10 (11:7–12:12)
Vayishlach	32:4–36:43	Hos. 11:7–12:12 (Obad. 1:1–21)
Vayeshev	37:1–40:23	Amos 2:6–3:8
Miketz	41:1–44:17	1 Kings 3:15–4:1
Vayigash	44:18–47:27	Ezek. 37:15–28
Vayechi	47:28–50:26	1 Kings 2:1–12
Exodus		
Shemot	1:1–6:1	Isa. 27:6–28:13; 29:22, 23 (Jer. 1:1–2:3)
Va'era	6:2–9:35	Ezek. 28:25–29:21
Bo	10:1–13:16	Jer. 46:13–28
Beshalach	13:17–17:16	Judg. 4:4–5:31 (5:1–31)

Name of Portion	Verses	Haftarah Portion
Yitro	18:1–20:23	Isa. 6:1–7:6; 9:5 (6:1–13)
Mishpatim	21:1–24:18	Jer. 34:8–22; 33:25, 26
Terumah	25:1–27:19	1 Kings 5:26–6:13
Teẓaveh	27:20–30:10	Ezek. 43:10–27
Ki Tisa	30:11–34:35	1 Kings 18:1–39 (18:20–39)
Vayak'hel	35:1–38:20	1 Kings 7:40–50 (7:13–26)
Pekudei	38:21–40:38	1 Kings 7:51–8:21 (7:40–50)
Leviticus		
Vayikra	1:1–5:26	Isa. 43:21–44:23
Tzav	6:1–8:36	Jer. 7:21–8:3; 9:22, 23
Sh'mini	9:1–11:47	2 Sam. 6:1–7:17 (6:1–19)
Tazria	12:1–13:59	2 Kings 4:42–5:19
Metẓora	14:1–15:33	2 Kings 7:3–20
Acḥarei Mot	16:1–18:30	Ezek. 22:1–19 (22:1–16)
Kedoshim	19:1–20:27	Amos 9:7–15 (Ezek. 20:2–20)
Emor	21:1–24:23	Ezek. 44:15–31
Behar	25:1–26:2	Jer. 32:6–27
Bechukotai	26:3–27:34	Jer. 16:19–17:14
Numbers		
Bamidbar	1:1–4:20	Hos. 2:1–22
Nasso	4:21–7:89	Judg. 13:2–25
Beha'alotcha	8:1–12:16	Zech. 2:14–4:7
Shelacḥ	13:1–15:41	Josh. 2:1–24
Koracḥ	16:1–18:32	I Sam. 11:14–12:22
Chukat	19:1–22:1	Judg. 11:1–33
Balak	22:2–25:9	Micah 5:6–6:8
Pincḥas	25:10–30:1	1 Kings 18:46–19:21
Mattot	30:2–32:42	Jer. 1:1–2:3
Massei	33:1–36:13	Jer. 2:4–28; 3:4 (2:4–28; 4:1, 2)

Name of Portion	Verses	Haftarah Portion
Deuteronomy		
Devarim	1:1–3:22	Isa. 1:1–27
Va'etchanan	3:23–7:11	Isa. 40:1–26
Ekev	7:12–11:25	Isa. 49:14–51:3
Re'eh	11:26–16:17	Isa. 54:11–55:5
Shoftim	16:18–21:9	Isa. 51:12–52:12
Ki Teteẓe	21:10–25:19	Isa. 54:1–10
Ki Tavo	26:1–29:8	Isa. 60:1–22
Nitẓavim	29:9–30:20	Isa. 61:10–63:9
Vayeilech	31:1–30	Isa. 55:6–56:8
Ha'azinu	32:1–52	2 Sam. 22:1–51
Vezot ha'Berachah	33:1–34:12	Josh. 1:1–18 (1:1–9)

APPENDIX B

Jewish Literature

Tanak

The *Tanak* includes twenty-four books that encompass the entire Old Testament, as some of the Christian Old Testament books are combined. Christians and Jews claim these books represent the divinely inspired Word of God. The word *Tanak* is an acronym taken from the first letters of the three major divisions of text: Torah, Neviim, and Kesuvim.[267] The Hebrew Tanak places the books in a slightly different order than the Christian Old Testament. Their order is as follows:

The five books of Moses (Chumash or Torah)
    Genesis
    Exodus
    Leviticus
    Numbers
    Deuteronomy

The eight books of the prophets *(Neviim)*
    Joshua
    Judges

---

[267] Daniel J. Hays and Tremper Longman III. *The Message of the Prophets: A Survey of the Prophetic and Apocalyptic Books of the Old Testament,* Kindle ed. Zondervan, 2010. Kindle locations 106–110.

Samuel (both 1 and 2 Samuel are combined into a single book)
Kings (both 1 and 2 Kings are combined into a single book)
Isaiah
Jeremiah
Ezekiel
The Twelve (this book includes the twelve minor prophets)

The Eleven Books of the Writings *(Kesuvim)*
  Psalms
  Proverbs
  Job
  Song of Songs
  Ruth
  Lamentations
  Ecclesiastes
  Esther
  Daniel
  Ezra/Nehemiah (both books are combined into one)
  Chronicles

Other rabbinic literature used to perpetuate understanding of Christian studies typically falls into one of four categories: Targumim, Mishna, Gemara, or Talmud.

Literature	Approximate Year Written
Targumim	AD 70 – Discovered in 1950s in Qumran
Mishna	AD 200
Gemara	AD 200–500
Talmud	AD 400–500

Midrash

Midrash is a form of rabbinic literature given in two forms: *midrash halakha*, which focuses on Jewish practice and the law, and *midrash aggada*, which focuses on the stories and how they might be interpreted. The word *midrash* comes from the Hebrew word *darash*, meaning "to inquire." Midrash is also known as *Mishnah*.

Mishnah

Rabbi Yehudah HaNasi wrote the Mishnah, originally the oral Torah, in its final form in approximately AD 200. He was the son of Simeon ben Gamaliel II, born AD 135 and died AD 219.[268] He was also known as Judah, Rebbi, or Rabbeinu HaKadosh. He finished the writing of the Mishnah in the town of Zippori.[269] Among the influential contributors were Rabbi Aqiba and his students.[270]

The Mishnah consists of chapter headings and main ideas only. It does not contain any dogmatic teachings. The Mishnah includes various opinions because it was intended to be a tool to teach the sages how to think through the questions of the Law rather than a specific code of law. It is fluid. Therefore, the principles would stay the same, but the applications would change based on circumstance. The text of the Mishnah quotes rabbis who lived from about 100 BC to AD 200. These rabbis include Rabbi Yochanan Ben Zakkai, Rabbi Shimon Bar Yochai, and Rabbi Akiba.

The whole Mishnah consists of six sections, sixty-three tractates, and 523 chapters. It is the cornerstone of Judaism.[271] Each tractate has fifty to one hundred Mishnayos (plural for Mishnah). It is interesting to see the unity in that the book as a whole has the name of a single element of its contents. The sixty-two sections are divided into six orders called *sedarim* and grouped based on content. The six orders are[272]

---

[268] Jewish Virtual Library. https://www.jewishvirtuallibrary.org/jsource/biography/hanasi.html (accessed March 29, 2014).

[269] Israel Ministry of Foreign Affairs. http://www.mfa.gov.il/mfa/israelexperience/history/pages/archaeological%20sites%20in%20israel%20-%20zippori.aspx (accessed March 29, 2014).

[270] Craig A. Evans. *Ancient Texts for New Testament Studies: A Guide to the BackgroundLiterature.* Reprint ed. Peabody, Massachusetts: Hendrickson Publishers, Inc., 2005, 221.

[271] Ibid., 221.

[272] Ibid.

- **Zera'im** ("seeds") – This tractate deals mostly with agricultural laws primarily applicable to life in Israel.
- **Mo'ed** ("feasts") – This tractate discusses the laws of the Sabbath and festivals.
- **Nasim** ("women") – This tractate deals with marriage and family law.
- **Neziqin** ("damages") – This tractate covers the court system, as well as civil and criminal law.
- **Qodasim** ("sacred things") – This tractate is focused on the temple and the divine service that was centered on the temple.
- **Tohorot** ("cleanliness") – This tractate discusses the laws of ritual purity.

Gemara

Commentary on the Mishnah accumulated for centuries and eventually culminated in the text of the Gemara. The Aramaic word *Gemara* means "tradition." In Hebrew, the word Gemara means "completion." Gemara, then, is a compilation of the various rabbinic dialogues on the Torah that completes the understanding of the Mishnah. The scholars who resided north of Jerusalem in Galilee were collecting commentaries at the same time as the scholars in Babylon were doing the same. The Jewish community in Babylon was more numerous and intellectual than in the Jerusalem area. This is evident in the size of the Gemara that came from each region.

The text of the Gemara quotes rabbis who lived from about AD 200 to approximately AD 500. These rabbis are called *amora'im* (explainers). The amora'im could not be ordained outside of Jerusalem, so the names of the Babylonian amora'im are usually preceded by the title *Rav* or *R'*. The amora'im of Israel carry the official title of rabbi or rebbe.

Other layers of text and commentaries from a later period surround the Gemara to form the Talmud.

Talmud

Cohen calls the Talmud "an intellectual enterprise for eternity."[273] It is the single most authoritative writing of Judaism. Its basic purpose is to provide guidelines for holy living.[274] It is part Mishnah and part Gemara. *Talmud* is the Hebrew word for "study," and it consists of twenty-four books. Those who study the Talmud read from it every day, and it takes them over seven years to complete.[275]

The writers of the Mishnah presumed that the reader would be familiar with its subject matter; thus, it is a bit cryptic in its shorthand style. As various interpretations of the Mishnah began to Hellenize the Scripture, the need for a standard commentary became obvious.

Jewish tradition says Ezra founded *Anshei Knesset HaGedolah* (The Great Assembly). These were the men who lived over three hundred years teaching and preserving Torah during the period between the Bible period (520 BC) and the Talmudic period (200 BC). The original Law was written by Moses and then handed to Joshua; Joshua gave it to the elders, the elders instructed the prophets, and in turn, these prophets became some of the men of the Great Assembly.

The Sanhedrin replaced the Great Assembly sometime in the third century BC. Josephus referred to the Sanhedrin as the senate.[276] Modern historical study, however, puts the Sanhedrin as descendants of Ezra; in addition, there were laymen along with the priests. As they discussed and even argued the somewhat trivial points of Mishnah, the priests would take a Hellenistic approach, even if it encouraged a lack of loyalty to the Torah. The laymen, on the other hand, vehemently opposed the priests in favor of Torah adherence.[277] The gap between them widened until two sects known as the Sadducees and Pharisees emerged. This controversy over the validity of the oral Torah was the beginning of the creation of the Talmud.[278]

---

[273] Cohen. *Everyman's Talmud,* 1996, foreword.

[274] Ibid., 149.

[275] Rabbi Michael Katz. *Swimming in the Sea of Talmud: Lessons for Everyday Living,* Kindle ed. Kindle locations 185–186.

[276] Josephus. *Antiquities* XII. III. 3.

[277] Josephus. *War* II. VIII. 14.

[278] Cohen. *Everyman's Talmud,* 1996, XXXIX.

Rav Ashe began the arduous task of compiling the Babylonian Talmud late in the third century. Upon his death in AD 427, after thirty years of work, Ravina I took over, and Ravina II eventually finished the Babylonian Talmud in AD 475. There was only minimal editing after AD 475 by Rabbanan Savura'i, and it was officially closed for editing in AD 476–560. Daniel Bomberg issued the first complete edition as it is known today in Venice. He produced the Babylonian Talmud in AD 1520–1523, while the Jerusalem Talmud was completed in 1523–1524.[279]

The two Talmuds have much in common. The Jerusalem Talmud was actually available to those in Babylon; thus, the commentary written for the Babylonian Talmud is articulated better, making it the authoritative text and the one used by most Jewish students.[280] Neither the Babylonian nor the Jerusalem Talmud contains the complete Gemara. The Jerusalem Talmud contains thirty-nine tractates, and the Babylonian contains thirty-seven tractates, although it is seven to eight times longer than the Jerusalem Talmud.[281]

The Talmud is largely a hypothetical debate, although some arguments written were actual debates conducted by the amora'im. For the most part, the controversies over the Torah that led to the compiling of the Talmud were trivial in nature. You would never hear arguments about important issues like kosher law or who should keep the laws about temple service. The matters up for argument were questions like "How long exactly is a Sabbath's day journey?" or "How long should one immerse oneself in a *mikvah* to be clean?" The sages understood that if they continued to bicker over the little things, they would soon lose any kind of unity, and without unity, they would be vulnerable to all their enemies.

The Talmud is an example of a critical literature review. The amora'ic rabbis actually encouraged the variety of interpretations. The scholars would present a particular viewpoint, and then they would make an argument for or against it using logical, elaborate, or incidental routes.

---

[279] Jewish Virtual Library. http://www.jewishvirtuallibrary.org/jsource/loc/Early.html (accessed April 5, 2014).
[280] Menachem Mendel Schneerson (Lubavithcher Rebbe) and Rabbi Jonathan Sacks. *Torah Studies: A Parsha Anthology.* Brooklyn: Kehot Publication Society, 2000, 14.
[281] Cohen. *Everyman's Talmud,* 1996, 1.

The Babylonian Talmud used other sources as well. In addition to Mishnah, the Babylonian Talmud includes other teachings of the authors of the Mishnah that were not included in the Mishnah itself. It also includes the teachings of the Jerusalem amora'im as well. There is teaching that is taken from nonlegal rabbinic teachings known as *Aggadah* that includes folklore and magical recipes.

Targumim

The word *Targum* means "translation" in Hebrew. While the Dead Sea Scrolls were written in Hebrew, Greek, and Aramaic, Targum refers specifically to the Aramaic portions of the Temple Scrolls.

In the caves of Qumran, it is believed that there lived a group of zealots called the Essenes.[282] Qumran is located west of the Dead Sea and north of Masada and En Gedi. Pliny the Elder describes this group of people as remarkable beyond all other tribes in the whole world, without money, women, or sexual desire.[283] Some teenaged shepherd boys found hundreds of scrolls in eleven caves in 1946–1947, over 220 Bible scrolls in all, including the Targumim. The mother lode of scrolls was found in 1952 in cave 4; however, it was not until 1956[284] that cave 11 exposed the Temple Scrolls. The single largest scroll discovered at Qumran measured twenty-eight feet in length.[285] This scroll included the Targum of Genesis, Targum of Leviticus, and two Targumim of Job.[286] It is not known for sure if the Essenes wrote the Targumim, but the consensus is that it was the work of the Essenes. There are different theories about how the manuscripts got into the caves at Qumran. The Essenes may have written them, they may have copied them, or perhaps they just had them in their possession.

---

[282] Josephus, Flavius and William Whiston, trans. *The Complete Works of Flavius Josephus: The Jewish War* (2.8.2–11). Kindle location 2468.

[283] *Jewish Encyclopedia*, ed., sv "Essenes." http://www.jewishencyclopedia.com/articles/5867-essenes (accessed May 20 2014).

[284] Evans. *Ancient Texts,* 2005, 133.

[285] Ibid., 135.

[286] Ibid., 149.

In any event, hiding them in the caves before the Romans attacked in AD 68 surely seems to indicate their theological convictions.[287]

I cannot go into detail about the Dead Sea scrolls and stay within the limits of this study; however, the discovery of the Targumim at Qumran is proof that the written Targumim were in circulation at the time of Jesus, a very important discovery for Christianity. Some scholars question whether John the Baptist could have been an Essene,[288] and others consider the similarities of Jesus' teaching with that of the Qumran community compelling.[289] Still others dismiss any similarities as unlikely and unsubstantive.[290]

Chumash

Chumash is merely a bound form of Sefer Torah, Torah that is on a scroll. *The Artscroll Chumash,* on the other hand, is Torah with a collection of classic rabbinic commentaries written by a team of Jewish scholars and edited by Rabbi Nosson Scherman. Commentaries in *The Artscroll Chumash* come from the Talmud, Midrash, and other commentators, including Rashi, Onkelos, and Sforno.

Gematria/Kabbalah

Gematria is a way of interpreting and applying the Torah. It is the philosophy of Torah. Oftentimes, it will discuss the use of the Hebrew language in numerical values and the implications of those values in relation to the plain meaning of the text. This system is popular among mystical followers of *kabbalah* (meaning the path of light). The ancient rabbis used Gematria to interpret the deeper meaning of the text. It is supposed to be mysterious and perplexing; however, it is common to see this concept blown out of

---

[287] James Vanderkam, Peter Flint. *The Meaning of the Dead Sea Scrolls: Their Significance for Understanding the Bible, Judaism, Jesus, and Christianity.* New York: Harper Collins Publishers, 2002, 255.

[288] Evans. *Ancient Texts,* 2005, 149.

[289] Ibid., 150–151.

[290] Walter A. Elwell and Robert W. Yarbrough. *Encountering Biblical Studies: Encountering the New Testament.* Grand Rapids: Baker Books, 2005, 58.

proportion. Some will use it to justify just about anything, usually in an attempt to sell you something that has nothing at all to do with Torah.[291]

Bahye ben Asher ibn Halawa, also known as Rabbeinu Bechayei (1340–1255), was the Jewish scholar and rabbi noted for introducing kabbalah into Torah study. He finds four methods imperative for proper exegesis of the Scripture, including *p'shat* (the plain meaning), the midrash or commentary on the text, logical analysis and philosophical exegesis (only insofar as it does not contradict the Torah or Jewish tradition), and finally, a soul who is on a search for truth. He believes when these are present, there are deep and hidden mysteries to be found in the Scriptures.[292]

Hasidic Judaism/Hasidism

Founded in the eighteenth century, *Hasidism* has the meaning of piety. This is a branch of Orthodox Judaism. Hasidic Jews promote Jewish mysticism as the foundation of faith. Baal Shem Tov (Israel ben Eliezer) wrote that he was the founder of Hasidic Judaism, claiming he received revelations from God during his long nightly walks alone in the forest.

Historical Theologians

Following is a brief synopsis of some of the historical theologians, sages, and rabbis revered today by the Jewish community. These authorities penned and compiled much of the literature I have used in my research. It is not my desire to include an exhaustive biography for each of these theologians; rather, the intent is to give credit to those whose work I have built upon in my search for applicable law and ultimate freedom in the life of a Christian. The scholars are listed in alphabetical order rather than importance or time.

Rabbi Abraham Ben Meir Ibn Ezra (AD 1089–1167): Known simply as Ibn Ezra, he was one of the most distinguished writers of the Middle

---

[291] Sara E. Karesh and Mitchell M. Hurvitz. *Encyclopedia of Judaism: Encyclopedia of World Religions,* Kindle ed. New York: Infobase Publishing, 2006. Kindle location 3838.

[292] Karesh and Hurvitz. *Encyclopedia of Judaism,* 2006. Kindle location 3838.

Ages. He was also a poet, astrologist, scientist, and Hebrew grammarian. Ibn Ezra introduced the decimal system using the Hebrew *alef* to *tet* for 1–9, but he added a special symbol to indicate zero. He wrote his most brilliant works during a self-exile as he wondered and pondered personal loss.[293]

Rabbi Akiba (AD 50–132): Akiba (or Akiva ben Joseph), a poor and semiliterate man, became one of Judaism's greatest scholars. He was a key player in the organization of the Mishnah. He also inspired Bar Kokhba to rebel against Rome in AD 131–135. When the rebellion failed, he was tortured to death by the Romans.[294]

Aquila (second century BC): He translated the Hebrew Scriptures into Greek. He was a Gentile at birth and followed the Christians for some time before converting to Judaism.[295]

Aristotle (384 BC–322 BC): Aristotle was a Greek philosopher and highly influential in the development of Western philosophy. He was a student of Socrates' philosophy, went to Plato's Academy, and tutored Alexander the Great.[296]

Rav Ashe (AD 352–427): He began the compilation of the Babylonian Talmud mentioned earlier in the section on Talmud.[297]

Rabbi Eliezer ben Hyrcanus (AD 40–120): Eliezer was one of five well-known disciples of Zakkai and teacher to Akiba.[298]

Hillel (32 BC–AD 7): Hillel was one of the most important people in Jewish history. Hillel was born in Babylon, died in Jerusalem, and was associated with the development of the Mishnah and Talmud. Some

---

[293] Bridger, David. *The New Jewish Encyclopedia*, ed., sv "Rabbi Abraham Ben Meir Ibn Ezra." West Orange: Behrman House Publishers, 1976, 216.

[294] Bridger, David. *The New Jewish Encyclopedia*, ed., sv "Rabbi Akiba." West Orange: Behrman House Publishers, 1976, 7.

[295] Jewish Encyclopedia.com, ed., sv "Aquila." http://www.jewishencyclopedia.com/articles/1674-aquila-akvlac-foreignchars-v02p034001-jpg-foreignchars (accessed May 7, 2014).

[296] Biography *Aristotle* http://www.biography.com/people/aristotle-9188415 (accessed June 6, 2014).

[297] Bridger, David. *The New Jewish Encyclopedia*, ed., sv "Rav Ashe." West Orange: Behrman House Publishers, 1976, 28.

[298] Nissan Mindel. *Rabbi Eliezer ben Hyrcanus.* http://www.chabad.org/library/article_cdo/aid/112309/jewish/Rabbi-Eliezer-Ben-Hyrkanos.htm.

compared Hillel to Moses, citing that both men lived 120 years; at the age of forty, Hillel went to Israel and studied for forty years. Finally, the last third of his life, he was the spiritual head of Israel, as was Moses. Hillel is known for the expression of *the ethic of reciprocity,* which states, "That which is hateful to you, do not do to your fellow. That is the whole Torah; the rest is the explanation; go and learn." From this, we derive the Golden Rule.[299]

Rabbi Israel ben Eliezer, also known as **Baal Shem Tov** (1698–1760): He wrote that he was the founder of Hasidic Judaism, arguably the most prominent religious movement in Jewish history. Baal Shem Tov means "Master of the Good Name," a designation reserved for holy men who were known to work miracles by the power of God. There is much uncertainty about the events in life, and even the year of his birth is debated.[300]

Josephus (AD 37–100): Titus Flavius Josephus, born Joseph ben Matityahu, was a first-century Roman/Jewish scholar and historian who was born in Jerusalem (at that time part of Roman Judea) to a father of priestly descent and a mother who claimed royal ancestry. He grew up as a contemporary of Jesus. Josephus was associated with the Essenes and later became a Pharisee. He wrote about history, emphasizing the first-century Jewish-Roman war including the last siege of Masada. Traditionally, he is thought to be a traitor, as he spent the last years of his life enjoying the many favors bestowed upon him by Roman emperors Vespasian and Titus.[301] His most important writings were *The Jewish War* (AD 75) and, in the year 94, *Antiquities of the Jews.* Although none of his work was included in the canon of Scripture, it has given great insight into Jewish culture and the Hebraic roots of Christianity.

R. Menachem Mendel Schneerson (1902–1994): The Lubavitcher Rebbe, also known simply as Rebbe, was a disciple of Rabbi Akiva. Rebbe was the seventh leader of Chabad-Lubavitch and lived in the Ukraine,

---

[299] Bridger, David. *The New Jewish Encyclopedia*, ed., sv "Hillel." West Orange: Behrman House Publishers, 1976, 206.

[300] Jewish Virtual Library. https://www.jewishvirtuallibrary.org/jsource/biography/baal.html (accessed May 20, 2014).

[301] Bridger, David. *The New Jewish Encyclopedia*, ed., sv "Josephus, Flavius." West Orange: Behrman House Publishers, 1976, 249.

Russia, Germany, Poland, France, and the United States. His commentaries are said to have changed Jewish life around the world.[302]

Rabbi Moses ben Maimon (1135–1204): Also known as **Maimonides**, and commonly referred to as **Rambam**, he is best known for his publication of the *Mishnah Torah* and the *Moreh Nevukhim* (Guide for the Perplexed).[303]

Rabbi Moses ben Naḥman (1194–1270): He was known to the non-Jewish world as Nachmanides and to the Jewish world as RamBan. Born to nobility and a student of Rabbi Judah ben Yakar, Ezra, and Aziel, he mastered the Talmud by the age of sixteen. He was the leading Jewish scholar of the medieval period. He was a doctor, philosopher, kabbalist, and commentator. He is best known for his last commentary on the Torah. He is well-known for his aggressive rebuttal of Christianity. His teachings were the first to incorporate kabbalah.[304]

Rabbi Nosson Scherman (1935–present): He was editor of *The Artscroll Chumash.*

Rabbi Obadiah ben Yaakov, also known as **Sforno** (1475–1550): He was born in Cesena, Italy. He taught the famous Christian scholar Johannes Reuchlin, and he wrote a philosophical book called *Or Ammim*. He also wrote an introduction to the commentary on the Torah, called "Kavonath Hatorah."[305] He is quoted often alongside Rashi, Rambam, Ibn Ezra, and Ramban.

Ohr HaChaim (1696–1743): Rabbi Chaim Ben Attar, known also as the Ohr Hachaim Hakadosh, only lived forty-seven years but made his mark as a great Talmudic scholar and was learned in kabbalah. His

[302] The Jewish Virtual Library, sv "R. Menachem Mendel Schneerson." https://www. jewishvirtuallibrary.org/jsource/biography/schneerson.html (accessed June 27, 2014).

[303] David Bridger. *The New Jewish Encyclopedia*, ed., sv "Rambam." West Orange: Behrman House Publishers, 1976, 301.

[304] Tracey Rich. *Judaism 101.* http://www.jewfaq.org/sages.htm (accessed May 20, 2014).

[305] Nissan Mindel. *Rabbi Obadiah Sforno.* Kehot Publication Society http://www. chabad.org/library/article_cdo/aid/111930/jewish/Rabbi-Obadiah-Sforno.htm (accessed May 20, 2014).

most important work was his commentary on the Torah, and he is often is published alongside Rashi and Rambam.[306]

Onkelos (AD 35–120): The great Onkelos translated the Torah into Aramaic. This text is called Targum Onkelos.[307] Onkelos was a member of the Roman royal family. His mother was Hadrian's sister and his father's name was Klonikas. According to the Babylonian Talmud, he was a proselyte who studied under Akiba.

Philo of Alexandria (20 BC–AD 50): Philo was an educated Hellenistic Jewish philosopher who grew up in Egypt. In an attempt to harmonize Greek philosophy and Jewish philosophy, he taught that Torah should be interpreted allegorically, as he felt a literal interpretation would stifle the finite perception of God, yet his articulation of Scripture is thought to be influenced by the apostles Paul and John. He is best known for his writing on history, commandments, and ethics of Judaism.[308]

Plato (428–423 BC to 348–347 BC): Plato was a Greek philosopher who wrote about Socrates. He was a student of Socrates and teacher to Aristotle. He was also a mathematician and founder of the first institution of higher learning located in Athens. His writings, related to the *Theory of Forms*, are referred to as Platonism. Many Platonic thoughts have influenced the Christian church, understanding that the forms that Platonism referred to were God's thoughts.[309]

Ravina I: Ravina I was an Amora. He edited the Gemara of the Babylonian Talmud until his death when Ravina II took it over.

Ravina II: Ravina II was an Amora. In AD 475–499, he finished editing the Gemara of the Babylonian Talmud. He was a student of Rav Ashi. He was also a nephew of Ravina I.

---

[306] Nissan Mindel. "Rabbi Chaim ibn Attar—(5456; 1696–1743)—Jewish History." Rabbi Chaim ibn Attar—(5456; 1696–1743)—Jewish History. http://www.chabad.org/library/article_cdo/aid/112384/jewish/Rabbi-Chaim-ibn-Attar.htm (accessed April 26, 2014).

[307] Bridger, David. *The New Jewish Encyclopedia*, ed., sv "Onkelos." West Orange: Behrman House Publishers, 1976, 361.

[308] Karesh and Hurvitz. *Encyclopedia of Judaism,* 2006. Kindle location 8318.

[309] David Sedley. *Plato's Cratylus: Cambridge Studies in the Dialogs of Plato,* 1st ed. New York: Cambridge University Press, 2003.

Samuel ben Meir (1083–1174; exact dates are uncertain): Also known as Rashbam, he was a grandson of the famous Rashi and one of the first *tosafot*. Like his grandfather, he taught the p'shat. Rashbam's most applicable teaching to the Christian is in his belief that one should always seek the p'shat, even when the Jewish traditions are challenged.[310]

Rabbi Shimon Bar Yohai: He is traditionally known as the author of the *Zohar*,[311] the central text of the kabbalah. He died on the thirty-third day of the Omer count, *LagBaOmer*. The date 18 Lyar in the Jewish calendar is set aside as a festival day to remember Shimon Bar Yochai. This festival, known as the Scholar's Holiday, also remembers the cessation of a plague and the oppression that made it life threatening to study or teach Torah.[312]

Rabbi Shimon Ben Gamliel I (AD 10–70): Gamliel was a descendant of the house of Hillel and president of the Sanhedrin AD 50–70, just before the destruction of the temple. He was a leader in the revolt against Rome and an adversary of Josephus, who believed that if Gamliel's orders had been followed consistently, the revolt against Rome would have been successful.[313] He is remembered by his philosophy of life. "There is nothing better than silence, and that he who talks much gives rise to sin. Not interpretation and study but work is the most virtuous thing."[314]

Rabbi Shlomo Yitzchaki, also known as **Rashi** (AD 1040–1105): Born in France, he is one of the most respected rabbis in Jewish history.[315] At age twenty-five, he founded his own academy in France. Rashi provided a simple explanation of the arguments of the Gemara. The first printed

---

[310] Rabbi Martin Lockshin. http://thetorah.com/rashbam-short-bio/ (accessed May 20, 2014).

[311] Bridger, David. *The New Jewish Encyclopedia*, ed., sv "Simeon Ben Yohai." West Orange: Behrman House Publishers, 1976, 451.

[312] Bridger, David. *The New Jewish Encyclopedia*, ed., sv "Simeon Ben Yohai." West Orange: Behrman House Publishers, 1976, 279.

[313] Shaye J. D. Cohen. *Josephus in Galilee and Rome: His Vita and Development as a Historian.* Boston: Brill Academic Publishers, 2002, 38.

[314] Zacharias Frankle. *Hodegetica in Mischnam, Librosqu Cum Ea Conjunctos Tosefta, Mechilta, Sifra, Sifrei (Vol. 1: Introductio in Mischnam).* Hunger, 1859, 63–64.

[315] Bridger, David. *The New Jewish Encyclopedia*, ed., sv "Rashi." West Orange: Behrman House Publishers, 1976, 399.

Bible text included Rashi's commentary, and this became so popular there are now more than two hundred commentaries on his commentary.[316]

Simon Ben Gamliel II: He was a descendant of the house of Hillel, adversary to Josephus, Tanna of the third generation, and president of the Great Sanhedrin and the college at Usha.[317]

Socrates (470 or 469 BC–399 BC): Socrates was an Athenian philosopher. He was indicted for impiety and corruption of youth and was condemned to death. He is generally considered one of the wisest men of all time, yet he is quoted as saying, "I know that I know nothing." He wrote nothing but is known by the writings of his students, primarily Plato and Xenophon.[318]

Yehudah HaNasi (AD 135–217): Yehudah HaNasi (meaning "Judah the Prince"), also known simply as Rebbe, was the son of Rabbi Shimon Ben Gamliel II. He was a great scholar, a strong leader, and a very wealthy man. The later years of his life were spent in the town of Tzipori (or Zippori), finishing the Mishnah in AD 190. It is also said that he won the favor of the Roman emperor Marcus Aurelius to the point that he acted as a counselor on personal matters as well as matters of state policy.[319]

Rabbi Yisroel Meir HaKohen (1838–1933): Also known as the Chofetz Chaim, he built upon the work of Rambam and identified seventy-seven positive and 194 negative commands that can be observed outside of Israel today. Rabbi Yisroel Meir published more than twenty books but is best known for his work on forbidden speech (Lashon Hara). His most important book was the Mishnah Berurah, which deals with the laws of daily life and holidays.[320]

---

[316] Jewish Virtual Library. https://www.jewishvirtuallibrary.org/jsource/biography/rashi.html (accessed April 30, 2014).

[317] Josephus. *War of the Jews*. Kindle location 6013.

[318] *Stanford Encyclopedia of Philosophy Socrates*. http://plato.stanford.edu/entries/socrates/ (accessed June 20, 2014).

[319] Rabbi Berel Wein. *Echoes of Glory: The Story of the Jews in the Classical Era*. Mesorah Publishing Ltd., 1995, 224.

[320] *The Chofetz Chaim—Rabbi Yisroel Meir HaKohen*. The Jewish Virtual Library. https://www.jewishvirtuallibrary.org/jsource/biography/chofetz.html (accessed June 27, 2014).

Yochanan ben Zakkai (first century AD): He was a disciple of Hillel, quoted often in the Mishnah, and the founder of the first rabbinic school at Yavneh called Sanhedrin.[321]

The Mishnah Torah

Mishnah Torah means "second law" and is used to describe the book of Deuteronomy. The Mishnah Torah is also the name given to the works of Rambam. The author of the Mishnah Torah is Rabbi Moshe ben Maimon, also known as Moses Maimonides and usually referred to by the acronym Rambam. He spent ten years of his life compiling the Mishnah Torah and the rest of his life revising it. It is divided into fourteen general sections, each of which is further subdivided into tractates and then into numbered chapters and laws.

Rambam identified 613 mitzvot in the Mishnah Torah. He divided them up into positive commands (i.e., love the Lord and honor your parents), and negative commands (you shall not covet …). Many of these mitzvot cannot be observed today; for example, many apply to the rules surrounding conduct and ritual in the temple; therefore, these mitzvot have not been applicable since the destruction of the temple in AD 70.[322]

Denominations of Judaism

Reformed   This is America's largest group. This movement began early in the nineteenth century in Germany. This group does not believe that the Scriptures are God given. Members believe that the Genesis account is something that the Israelites imagined creation to be like. They believe that every generation has the right to accept only the laws that they feel are essential and can therefore reject any laws they feel would be frivolous, such as the dietary laws, the covering of one's head in the synagogue,

---

[321] Karesh and Hurvitz. *Encyclopedia of Judaism,* 2006. Kindle location 3611.

[322] Dan Juster. *Jewish Roots,* 1995, 259–287.

or restraining from work on the Sabbath. Unlike previous generations, today the reformed Jews celebrate traditional holidays and honor the guidelines known as The Pittsburg Platform. This denomination of Judaism encourages Hebrew and Torah study, observance of Shabbat, and the importance of the mitzvot.[323]

Conservative

The Conservative movement has a wide range of observances. It began in the United States in the late nineteenth century as a result of the growing dissatisfaction in the Orthodox synagogue service and the Reform movement. This group accepts the doctrine of divine inspiration of the Scriptures to a point. It is that point that can vary with the denomination. As a general rule, members keep the dietary laws, the Sabbath, and traditions as much as possible.[324]

Reconstructive

Reconstructionism is the most modern denomination of Judaism and was started in New York by Rabbi Mordecai Kaplan. To this group of people, Judaism is more than a religion; it is a way of life. The emphasis is placed on Jewish tradition and the survival of the Jewish community.[325]

Orthodox

Orthodox Judaism originally referred to the historic religion of the Jewish people, but since the rise of the Reform denomination, it specifically refers to those who hold to strict traditional Jewish beliefs. This group is well educated in Torah and ritual observance. Members follow closely the ethics and the commentary recorded by the Tanaim and

---

[323] Bridger. *The New Jewish Encyclopedia*, 1976, 402.
[324] Ibid., 96.
[325] Ibid., 401.

amora'im. They believe in the literal doctrine of revelation. They are devoted to daily prayer of Shema, dietary laws, observance of the Sabbath, celebration of the feasts and the fasts, and laws of family purity. They are required to live pious, righteous, and charitable life.[326] This group is easily recognizable at prayer time by the wearing of the tallit, tefillin, and tzitzit.

Secular Humanist   Secular humanists are a small sect of atheists who believe in Judaism as a cultural people. They have temples and ordain rabbis but do not follow any traditional observances.[327]

Jewish Renewal   In an attempt to regain the lost Jews, this sect has integrated more meditation, hand-holding, chanting, and singing. Members add kabbalah and other popular, even secular, elements to the services. This group is compared to the seeker-friendly church of the Christians.[328]

Messianic   Messianic Judaism is a grassroots movement among Jewish and non-Jewish believers of Jesus Christ who recognize the Jewishness of Jesus and Jesus as their roots. This movement first appeared in the late 1960s and is now gaining much popularity because of how it blends the evangelical Christian theology with traditional Jewish practice. Most messianic Jews

---

[326] Bridger. *The New Jewish Encyclopedia*, 1976, 363.

[327] Debra Nussbaum Cohen. *Judaism with No God: A Look at the Challenges and Opportunities Facing Secular Humanism.* http://www.myjewishlearning.com/history/Jewish_World_Today/Denominations/Secular_Humanism.shtml?HSTY (accessed May 20, 2014).

[328] Debra Nussbaum Cohen. *Jewish Renewal: An Introduction to the Jewish Renewal Movement.* http://www.myjewishlearning.com/history/Jewish_World_Today/Denominations/Renewal_Movement.shtml?HSTY (accessed May 20, 2014).

hold to Trinitarian beliefs, though there are some exceptions. Trinitarians hold to the belief that God the Father, God the Son, and God the Spirit are the One True God, three in one. According to The Chosen People Ministries, there are over two hundred messianic congregations in the United States.[329] It has been reported that there are more than 150 in Israel with an estimated 20,000 members.[330]

Messianic Organizations

Messianic Judaism is a religious movement that blends Jewish tradition and ritual with the theological beliefs of evangelical Christianity. Although the messianic Jewish church began at Pentecost fifty days after Passover, also known as The Feast of Weeks, it gained popularity in the 1960s and 1970s. The first known messianic Jews were known as the Elkesaites (around the second century), in reference to the prophet Elkesai. These messianic Jews practiced kosher laws, engaged in frequent immersions for purification, and were often thought of as heretics.[331] Today, there are more than one hundred and fifty messianic congregations in the Holy Land of Israel with more than twenty thousand Jewish believers of Jesus. Globally those numbers are thought to be upward of three hundred thousand messianic Jewish believers.[332] Some of the popular messianic Jewish organizations include the following:

- The Messianic Jewish Alliance of America (MJAA)
- Union of Messianic Jewish Congregations (UMJC), focusing on the relational unity of Jews and Gentiles

---

[329] Mitch Glaser. *Jewish Roots*. http://www.chosenpeople.com/main/jewish-roots/304-messianic-congregations-and-the-modern-messianic-movement (accessed March 29, 2014).

[330] Jewish Israel. *Statistics*. http://jewishisrael.ning.com/page/statistics-1 (accessed March 29, 2014).

[331] Everett Ferguson. *Backgrounds of Early Christianity*, 3rd ed. Grand Rapids: William B. Eerdmans Publishing Company, 2003, 614.

[332] Jewish Israel, *Statistics* (accessed March 29, 2014).

- Messianic Israel Alliance (with over 130 congregations and ministries)
- Chosen People Ministries (CPM), focusing on the compatibility of Jesus and Judaism
- Coalition of Torah Observant Messianic Congregations (CTOMC)
- International Federation of Messianic Jews (IFMJ)
- Union of Conservative Messianic Synagogues (UCMJS)
- The International Alliance of Messianic Congregations and Synagogues (IAMCS)
- HaYesod ("The Foundation")
- The Jerusalem Council
- The Messianic Jewish Rabbinical Council
- Beth Immanuel Sabbath Fellowship
- Kehilat Sar Shalom
- Seed of Abraham Messianic Congregation
- Corner Fringe Hebrew Roots Congregation
- Tabernacle of David

BIBLIOGRAPHY

Aidekman, Gary. "Why Areyvut Is So Important to Me." Speak EZ. February 2011. 1 Voice of UJC Leadership. http://jfedgmw.org/page. aspx?id=237417.

Alter, Robert. *The Five Books of Moses: A Translation with Commentary.* New York: W. W. Norton & Company, 2008.

Aquinas, St. Thomas. *On Prayer and the Contemplative Life,* Kindle ed. S.I.:General Books, 2009.

Archer, Gleason L. *A Survey of Old Testament: Introduction.* Chicago: Moody Press, 1994.

Aristotle. *Rhetoric,* translated by W. Rhys Roberts, Kindle ed. Publish This, LLC. 2007.

Arnold, Bill T. and Bryan E. Beyer. *Encountering the Old Testament, a Christian Survey.* Grand Rapids: Baker Books, 1999.

Artson, Rabbi Bradley Shavit, and Rabbi Patricia Fenton. "Walking with God: Mitzvot Ha-Teluyot Ba'aretz U8:5–6." Ziegler School of Rabbinic Studies. http://ziegler.aju.edu/default.aspx?id=5188.

Augustine, St. and Wyatt North, trans. *The Life and Writings of Saint Augustine,* Kindle ed. Wyatt North Publishing, 2012.

Blair, E. P. *An Appeal to Remembrance: The Memory Motif in Deuteronomy.* Int 15 1961.

Blech, Rabbi Benjamin. *Selfies: The Word of the Year.* http://www.aish.com/ci/s/Selfies-The-Word-of-the-Year.html.2013.

Block, Daniel I. *How I Love Your Torah, O LORD! Studies in the Book of Deuteronomy.* Eugene, Oregon: Cascade Books, 2011.

Bloch. Sha'are. http://www.jewishencyclopedia.com/articles/12390-prosbul. 2014.

Brauner, Reuven. *613 Commandments in Prose: Eclectic Torah Compilations.* Raanana, Israel: Talmudic Books, 2012.

_____. *An Adaption of the Rosh's Sefer Orchos Chayim: The Pathways of Life.* Raanana, Israel: Talmudic Books, 2012.

_____. *Laws of Kings and Wars: Translations from Rambam's Mishne Torah. (Eclectic Torah Compilations).* Raanana, Israel: Talmudic Books, 2012.

Brawer, Naftali. *A Brief Guide to Judaism: Theology, History, and Practice,* Kindle ed. London: Robinson, 2013.

Bridger, David, and Samuel Wolk. *The New Jewish Encyclopedia.* Revised ed. West Orange: Behrman House, 1976.

Brown, Michael L. *60 Questions Christians Ask about Jewish Beliefs and Practices.* Bloomington, Minnesota: Baker Publishing Group, 2011.

Bruce, F. F. *The Cannon of Scripture.* Downers Grove: InterVarsity Press, 1988.

Bullock, Hassell. JETS 52/1. March 15, 2009. *Wisdom, the "Amen" of Torah.* Franklin S. Dyrness, professor of biblical studies at Wheaton

College, delivered this presidential address at the sixtieth annual meeting of the ETS in Providence, Rhode Island, on November 20, 2008.

Chabad-Lubavitch Media Center: Under the Auspices of the Lubavitch World Headquarters. "Today in Judaism." Chabadorg RSS. http://www.chabad.org 2014.

Glaser, Dr. Mitch. "Chosen People Ministries." http://www.chosenpeople.com/main 2014.

Campenhausen, Hans von. *The Formation of the Christian Bible.* London: Augsburg Fortress Publishing, 1972.

Chinitz, Jacob. "The Word Torah in the Torah." *Jewish Bible Quarterly,* Vol. 33, No 4, 2005.

Clinton, Boruch. *Midrash: Bringing Torah to Life.* Canada: Marbitz Media, Kindle ed. 2012.

Coffman, Elesha. *Christian History "Why December 25?"* http://www.christianitytoday.com/ch/news/2000/dec08.html.2014.

Cohen, Abraham. *Everyman's Talmud: The Major Teachings of the Rabbinic Sages.* Reprint ed. New York: Schocken Books Inc., 1996.

Cohen, A. and A. Mishcon. *Soncino Babylonian Talmud: Abodah Zarah,* Kindle ed. Teaneck: Talmudic Books, 2012.

_____. *Soncino Babylonian Talmud Sotah,* Kindle ed. Teaneck: Talmudic Books, 2012.

Cohen, Debra Nussbaum. *Jewish Renewal: An Introduction to the Jewish Renewal Movement* http://www.myjewishlearning.com/history/Jewish_World_Today/Denominations/Renewal_Movement.shtml? HSTY. 2014.

Cohen, Shaye J. D. *Josephus in Galilee and Rome: His Vita and Development as a Historian*. Boston: Brill Academic Publishers, 2002.

Collins, John J. *The Transformation of the Torah in Second Temple Judaism: Journal for the Study of Judaism* 43, 2012.

Comes, Arthur. "Motivation and the Growth of Self." *Perceiving, Behaving, and Becoming: The Association for Supervision and Curriculum Development Yearbook*. Washington, DC: National Education Association, 1962.

Daiches, Samuel and Israel W. Slotki. *Soncino Babylonian Talmud Kethuboth,* Kindle ed. Teaneck, New Jersey: Talmudic Books, 2012.

Davis, Avronhom. *Metsudah Midrash Tanchuma Devorim,* Monsey: Metsudah Publications, 2004.

DeHaan, M. D. *The Tabernacle.* Grand Rapids: Zondervan Publishing, 1955.

Dictionary.com, LLC, sv "Tripping," http://dictionary.reference.com/browse/tripping 2010.

_____, sv "Idiom," http://dictionary.reference.com/browse/idiom?s=t; 2014.

Dillard, Raymond B., Tremper Longman. *An Introduction to the Old Testament.* Grand Rapids: Zondervan, 2006.

Donin, Rabbi Hayim Halevy. *To Pray as a Jew: A Guide to the Prayer Book and Synagogue Service,* Kindle ed. New York: Basic Books, 2001.

Eisenberg, Ronald L. *The 613 Mitzvot: A Contemporary Guide to the Commandments of Judaism,* Kindle ed. Shengold Publishers, Schreiber Publishing, 2012.

Elias, Joseph. *The World of Rabbi Hirsch: The Nineteen Letters.* 2nd *ed.* Jerusalem: Feldheim Publishers, 1996.

Elwell, Walter A., Robert W. Yarbrough. *Encountering Biblical Studies: Encountering the New Testament.* Grand Rapids: Baker Books, 2005.

Evans, Craig A. *Ancient Texts for New Testament Studies: A Guide to the Background Literature.* Reprint ed. Peabody, Massachusetts: Hendrickson Publishers, Inc., 2005.

Fee, Gordon D., and Douglas Stuart. *How to Read the Bible for All It's Worth.* Nashville: Zondervan, 2003.

Feinberg, Jeffrey Enoch. *Walk Genesis! A Messianic Jewish Devotional Commentary; for Readers of the Torah, Haftarah, and B'rit Chadashah.* Clarksville: Lederer Books, a division of Messianic Jewish Publishers, 1998.

Ferguson, Everett. *Backgrounds of Early Christianity.* 3rd ed. Grand Rapids: William B. Eerdmans Publishing Company, 2003.

Fishbane, M. "From Scribalism to Rabbinism." *The Sage in Israel and the Ancient Near East,* ed. J. G. Gammie. Winona Lake, Indiana: Eisenbrauns, 1990.

Flannery, Austin. *Declaration on the Relation of the Church to Non-Christian Relations,* in *Vatican II: The Conciliar and Post-Conciliar Documents,* vol. 1, ed. Collegeville, Minnesota: Liturgical Press, 1984.

Frankel, Zacharias. *Hodegetica in Mischnam: Librosqu cum Ea Conjunctos Tosefta, Mechilta, Sifra, Sifrei (Vol. 1: Introductio in Mischnam).* Hungary, 1859.

Freedman, H. *Soncino Babylonian Talmud Pesahim,* Kindle ed. Teaneck: Talmudic Books, 2012.

_____. *Soncino Babylonian Talmud Shabbath,* Kindle ed. Teaneck: Talmudic Books, 2012.

Geisler, Norman L. *Chosen but Free: A Balanced View of Divine Election.* Minneapolis: Bethany House Publishers, 2001.

Ginzberg, Louis. *The Legends of the Jews.* Henrietta Szold trans., Kindle ed. Philadelphia: Jewish Publication Society of America, 2010.

Grunlan, Stephen A., and Marvin K. Mayers. *Cultural Anthropology: A Christian Perspective.* Grand Rapids: Zondervan, 1979.

"Guidelines for Jewish-Christian Relations," issued by the 1988 General Convention. Regarding teachings from the Anglican Communion, see "Jews, Christians and Muslim: The Way of Dialogue," appendix 6 of the Report of the Dogmatic and Pastoral Section by the 1998 Lambeth Conference.

Gundry, Patricia. *Woman Be Free: Biblical Equality for Women.* Grand Rapids: Smith Gundry Publications, 1977.

Halivni, David Weiss. *Midrash, Mishnah, and Gemara: The Jewish Predilection for Justified Law.* Cambridge, Massachusetts: Harvard University Press, 1986.

Hammer, Reuven. *The Classic Midrash: Tannaitic Commentaries on the Bible, Classics of Western Spirituality.* 1st ed. Mahwah, New Jersey: Paulist Press, 1995.

Hans von Campenhausen. *The Formation of the Christian Bible.* London: Augsburg Fortress Publishing, 1972.

Harris, Maurice. Hebraic Literature: Translations from the Talmud, Midrashim and *Kabbala,* Kindle ed. New York: Tudor Publishing Company, 2012.

Hays, J. Daniel and Longman III, Tremper. *The Message of the Prophets: A Survey of the Prophetic and Apocalyptic Books of the Old Testament*, Kindle ed. Grand Rapids: Zondervan, 2010.

Heidebrecht, Vern. *Hearing God's Voice: Eight Keys to Connecting with God*, Kindle ed. Colorado Springs: David C Cook, 2010.

Heschel, Abraham Joshua. *God in Search of Man: A Philosophy of Judaism*. New York: Farrar, Straus, and Giroux, 1983.

Huey, William Mark and J. K. McKee. *Hebraic Roots: An Introductory Study*. Downers Richardson: TNN Press, a division of Outreach Israel Ministries, 1992.

_____. *Counting the Omer: A Daily Devotional toward Shavu'ot*, Kindle ed. Richardson: TNN Press, 2011.

Israel Ministry of Foreign Affairs. http://www.mfa.gov.il/mfa/israel experience/history/pages/archaeological%20sites%20in%20israel%20 -%20zippori.aspx.

Israel Ministry of Foreign Affairs. http://mfa.gov.il/mfa/Pages/default.aspx 2014.

Israelstam, J., M. H. Segal, and H. M. Lazarus. *Soncino Babylonian Talmud Makkoth, Eduyyoth and Aboth*, Kindle ed. Teaneck: Talmudic Books, 2012.

Jacobson, Simon. *Toward a Meaningful Life, New Edition: The Wisdom of the Rebbe Menachem Mendel Schneerson*, Kindle ed. HarperCollins, 2010.

Jewish Encyclopedia.com. 1906 Edition. West Conshohocken, Pennsylvania, 2011. http://www.jewishencyclopedia.com.

Jewish Israel, administrative director: Avraham Leibler, Academic and Religious Advisor: Rabbi Dr. Jeffrey R. Woolf. http://jewishisrael. ning.com/.2014.

Jewish Virtual Library. 2014. http://www.jewishvirtuallibrary.org/index.html.

Josephus, Flavius. *Antiquities of the Jews: The Complete Works of Flavius Josephus,* Kindle ed. Translated by William Whiston.

_____. *War of the Jews: The Complete Works of Flavius Josephus,* Kindle ed. Translated by William Whiston.

Joslyn-Siemiatkoski, Daniel. *Moses Receives the Torah at Sinai and Handed It On (Michnah Avot 1:1): The Relevance of the Written and Oral Torah for Christians.* American Theological Library Association ATR/91:3.

Jukes, Andrew. *The Law of the Offerings.* Counted Faithful Publishing, Kindle ed., 2012.

Jung, Leo and Maurice Simon, and L. Miller. *Soncino Babylonian Talmud Bekoroth and Arakin,* Kindle ed. Talmudic Books, 2012.

Juster, Dan. *Jewish Roots: A Foundation of Biblical Theology.* Shippensburg, Pennsylvania: Destiny Image Messianic, 1995.

Kagan, Rabbi Yisrael Meir and Rabbi Shraga Silerstein. *Chafetz Chaim,* Kindle ed. Jerusalem: Silverstein, 2014.

Kaiser, Walter C. Jr. *Toward an Old Testament Theology.* Grand Rapids: Zondervan, 1979.

Katz, Rabbi Michael and Gershon Schwartz. *Swimming in the Sea of Talmud: Lessons for Everyday Living,* Kindle ed. Philadelphia: The Jewish Publication Society, 1998.

Karesh Sara E. and Mitchell M. Hurvitz. *Encyclopedia of Judaism Encyclopedia of World Religions,* Kindle ed. New York: Infobase Publishing, 2006.

Kent, Keri Wyatt. *Deeper into the Word: New Testament.* "A Disciple of Rabbi Jesus: Exploring the Meaning of Disciple." Bethany House Publishers. http://www.smallgroups.com/articles/2012/disciplerabbijesus.html2011.

Kingscote, Robert F. *Christ as Seen in the Offerings,* Kindle ed. Bible Truth Publishers, 2011.

Kirzner, E. W. *Soncino Babylonian Talmud Baba Kamma,* Kindle ed. Teaneck: Talmudic Books, 2012.

Kline, Meredith. *Treaty of the Great King: The Covenant Structure of Deuteronomy: Studies and Commentary.* Eerdmans: Wipf & Stock Pub, 1963.

Klien, B. D. *Soncino Babylonian: Talmud Nazir,* Kindle ed. Teaneck: Talmudic Books, 2012.

Klein, William W., Craig L. Blomberg, and Robert L. Hubbard. *Introduction to Biblical Interpretation.* Nashville: Thomas Nelson, Inc., 2004.

Leibowitz, Yeshayahu. *Accepting the Yoke of Heaven.* Jerusalem: Urim Publications, 2006.

Levy, David M. *The Tabernacle: Shadows of the Messiah: Its Sacrifices, Services, and Priesthood.* Grand Rapids: Kregel Publications, 2003.

Luther, Martin. *An Open Letter on Translating,* Kindle ed. Public Domain Books. Translated from "Sendbrief von Dolmetschen" in _Dr. Martin Luthers Werke_, (Weimar: Hermann Boehlaus Nachfolger, 1909), Band 30, Teil II, pp. 632–646 by Gary Mann, Ph.D. 2009.

_____. *Concerning Christian Liberty,* Kindle ed. Public Domain Books. 2006.

_____. *How Christians Should Regard Moses, in Luther Works, vol. 35, Word and Sacrament,* ed. Helmut T. Lehmann and E. Theodore Bachman. Philadelphia: Muhlenberg Press, 1960.

_____. *Treatise on Good Works.* 1520, Kindle ed., 2014.

Mayer, John. "Church History: Cityview Report," Interviewed by Donna Stundahl, Maple Plain, Minnesota, June 1, 2014.

McConville J. G. and J. G. Millar. *Time and Place in Deuteronomy.* Sheffield, England: Sheffield Academic Press, 1994.

Malina, Bruce J. *The New Testament World: Insights from Cultural Anthropology.* Louisville: Westminster John Knox Press. 2001.

Merrill, Eugene II. *The New American Commentary: An Exegetical and Theological Exposition of the Holy Scripture, Volume 4 Deuteronomy.* Nashville: B&H Publishing, Kindle ed., 1994.

Messer, Rabbi Ralph. *Torah: Law or Grace?* "Kingdom Principles for Kingdom Living," Kindle ed. STBM Publishing. 2011.

Michael, Boaz. *First Fruits of Zion.* https://ffoz.com/about-our-company.html 2014.

Mishnah. *Ethics of the Fathers (Pirkei Avot).* http://www.chabad.org/library/article_cdo/aid/682516/jewish/English-Text.htm.

Nathan, de-Rabbi, translator. *Avot: The Fathers According to Rabbi Nathan, Judah Goldin.* New Haven, Connecticut: Yale University Press, 1955.

Nissan Mindel. *Rabbi Obadiah Sforno* Kehot Publication Society. http://www.chabad.org/library/article_cdo/aid/111930/jewish/Rabbi-Obadiah-Sforno.htm.2014.

Noll, Mark A. *Turning Points: Decisive Moments in the History of Christianity* 3rd. ed. Grand Rapids: Baker Academic, 2012.

North, Wyatt. *The Life and Writings of Saint Augustine,* Kindle ed. Wyatt North Publishing, 2012.

Olukoya, Dr. D. K. *The Mystery of First Fruit Offering,* Kindle ed. Sabo-Yaba: The Battle Cry Christian Ministries, 2007.

Parsons, John. *Behold the Goat of God! Yeshua as Korban Ha'Olam, Hebrew for Christians.* http://www.hebrew4christians.com/Holidays/Fall_Holidays/Yom_Kippur/Goat_of_God/goat_of_god.html, 2014.

_____. *Elul and Selichot: The Season of Teshuvah—Hebrew for Christians.* http://www.hebrew4christians.com/Holidays/Fall_Holidays/Elul/Elul.pdf, 2014.

_____. *Every Letter of Torah: Further Thoughts on Parashat Haberakhah* Hebrew For Christians. http://www.hebrew4christians.com/Scripture/Parashah/Summaries/Vzot-Haberakhah/Letter/letter.html, 2014.

_____. La'asok be'divrei Torah: Customary Blessing before Torah Study. http://www.hebrew4christians.net/Blessings/Daily_Blessings/Torah_Study/torah_study.html, 2014.

_____. *Teshuvah and Creation,* Hebrew for Christians. http://hebrew4christians.com/Holidays/Fall_Holidays/Elul/Creation/creation.html, 2014.

Piper, John. *What Jesus Demands from the World.* Wheaton: Crossway Books, 2006.

Rabbinowitz, Joseph. *Soncino Babylonian Talmud: Taanith*, Kindle ed. Teaneck: Talmudic Books, 2012.

Rambam. Translated by Rabbi Berel Bell. *Sefer HaMitzvos of the Rambam Volume 1,* Kindle ed. Brooklyn: Sichos In English, 2013.

Rambam, Maimonides, Moses; Franck, Adolphe. Translated by M. Friedlander. *The Guide for the Perplexed & the Kabbalah or the Religious Philosophy of the Hebrews,* Kindle ed., 2012.

Rich, Tracey R. *Judaism 101.* http://www.jewfaq.org/index.shtml. 2014.

Rogers, Carl. *Freedom to Learn for the 80's.* Columbus, Ohio: Merill, 1983.

Rose, Tov. *The Paranormal Seams of the Hebrew Bible,* Kindle ed., 2012.

Rosenfeld, Dovid. *Mishna, Pirkei Avos 1:4.* Beit Shamesh, Israel. http://www.torah.org/learning/pirkei-avos/chapter1-4.html, 2014.

_____. *Can Man Destroy the World?* Mishna 3.19a. http://www.torah.org/learning/pirkei-avos/chapter3-19a.html. 2014.

Ryken, Leland. *How to Read the Bible as Literature.* 7th ed. Grand Rapids: Zondervan, 1984.

Ryrie, Charles C. *A Survey of Bible Doctrine,* Kindle ed. Chicago: Moody Publishers, 1989.

_____. *Basic Theology: A Popular Systematic Guide to Understanding Biblical Truth,* Kindle ed. Chicago: Moody Publishers, 1999.

_____. *Dispensationalism Today.* Chicago: Moody Press, 1965.

Sassoon, Isaac and Isaac D. D. Sassoon. *Destination Torah: Notes and Reflections on Selected Verses from the Weekly Torah Readings.* Jersey City: Ktav Pub Inc., 2001.

Saucy, Robert. *The Case for Progressive Dispensationalism: The Interface between Dispensational and Non-Dispensational Theology*, Kindle ed. Grand Rapids: Zondervan, 2010.

Scherman, Rabbi Nosson and Rabbi Meir Zlotowitz. *The Chumash: Artscroll Series*. Stone Edition. New York: Mesorah Publications, 2000.

Schneerson, Rabbi Menachem Mendel, and Rabbi Jonathan Sacks. *Torah Studies: A Parsha Anthology*. Brooklyn: Kehot Publication Society, 2000.

Schneerson, Rabbi Menachem Mendel. Translated by Chassida Halevi. *Good Advice: 50 Suggestions for a Good Life*. Jewish Wisdom Collection, Kindle ed. Israel: Ruach Nachon Publishing House, 2013.

Scott, Bruce. *The Feasts of Israel: Seasons of the Messiah*, Friends of Israel Gospel Ministry, Inc. 1997.

Schreiner, Thomas and Benjamin Merkle. *40 Questions about Christians and Biblical Law (40 Questions & Answers Series)*. Grand Rapids: Kregel Publications, 2010.

Sedley, David. *Plato's Cratylus (Cambridge Studies in the Dialogues of Plato)*, Kindle ed. Cambridge University Press, 2003.

Shachter, Jacob and Freedman, H. *Soncino Babylonian Talmud Sanhedrin*, Kindle ed. Teaneck: Talmudic Books, 2012.

Silbermann, Rabbi M. *Pentateuch with Targum Onkelos and Rashi's Commentary: Torah, the Book of Devarim*. Volume V (Hebrew / English). Middletown: BN Publishing, 2011.

Simon, Maurice. *Soncino Babylonian Talmud: Rosh Hashanah*, Kindle ed. Teaneck: Talmudic Books, 2012.

Simon, Maurice. *Soncino Babylonian Talmud: Berakoth*, Kindle ed. Teaneck: Talmudic Books, 2012.

Simon, Maurice. *Soncino Babylonian Talmud Gittin*, Kindle ed. Teaneck: Talmudic Books, 2012.

Simon, Maurice and Moses Hirsch Segal. *Soncino Babylonian Talmud Megillah and Shekalim*, Kindle ed. Teaneck: Talmudic Books, 2012.

Rabbi Shraga Simmons. *ABC's of Yom Kippur.* http://www.aish.com/h/hh/yom-kippur/guide/ABCs-of-Yom-Kippur.html, 2014.

Slavin, Robert E. *Educational Psychology: Theory and Practice.* Boston: Allyn & Bacon, 1994.

Slotki, Israel W. and Maurice Simon. *Soncino Babylonian Talmud Baba Bathra*, Kindle ed. Teaneck: Talmudic Books, 2012.

Slotki, Israel W. *Soncino Babylonian Talmud Sukkah, Kindle* ed. Teaneck: Talmudic Books, 2012.

Soulen, R. Kendall. *The God of Israel and Christian Theology.* Minneapolis: Fortress Press, 1996.

Steinsaltz, Adin. *The Essential Talmud.* New York: Random House Inc., 2006.

Stern, David H., translator. *Jewish News Testament.* Clarksville, Maryland: Jewish New Testament Publication, 1989.

Stern, PhD, David H. *Restoring the Jewishness of the Gospel: A Message for Christians Condensed from Messianic Judaism,* Kindle ed. Clarksville: Lederer Books, 2009.

Steyer, Rabbi Ute, MA. *A Different Interpretation of Hester Panim.* The Jewish Theological Seminary, 2014.

Strong, James. *The Tabernacle of Israel: Its Structure and Symbolism.* Grand Rapids: Kregel Publications, 1987.

Swindoll, Charles R. and Roy B. Zuck. *Understanding Christian Theology.* Nashville: Thomas Nelson Publishers, 2003.

The Torah.com. *A Historical and Contextual Approach.* Professor Marc Zvi Brettler and Rabbi David D. Steinberg, founders. http://thetorah.com.

Tigay, Jeffrey H. *JPS Torah Commentary: Deuteronomy.* Philadelphia: Jewish Publication Society, 1996.

Torah.org, Project Genesis, Inc. Director Rabbi Yaakov Menken. http://www.torah.org/2007.

Vander Laan, Ray. That the World May Know Ministries. *The Rabbi and His Talmidim.* (2003) http://followtherabbi.com/guide/detail/rabbi-and-talmidim.pdf, 2014.

Vanderkam, James and Peter Flint. *The Meaning of the Dead Sea Scrolls: Their Significance for Understanding the Bible, Judaism, Jesus, and Christianity.* New York: Harper Collins Publishers, 2002.

Vassar, John. "A Conversation with John Vassar." Interviewed by author. Maple Plain, February 16, 2013.

Virkler, Henry A., and Karelynne Gerber Ayayo. *Hermeneutics: Principles and Processes of Biblical Interpretation.* Grand Rapids: Baker, 1981, 2007.

Webb, Brian Thomas. *Strongs Exhaustive Concordance of the Bible.* Version 1.5.3 for iPhone 2009.

Webb, Dr. Katheryn. *Madeline Hunter Dynamic Teaching.* Trinity Collage of the Bible Theological Seminary, 2008.

Wein, Rabbi Berel. *Echoes of Glory: The Story of the Jews in Classical Era.* Brooklyn: Mesorah Publishing Ltd, 1995.

Wolpe, David. *Hester Panim in Modern Jewish Thought, Modern Judaism 17.1* The Johns Hopkins University Press, 1997.

Wright, Christopher J. H. *Knowing Jesus through the Old Testament.* Downers Grove: InterVarsity Press, 1992.

Wright, N. T. *Justification: God's Plan & Paul's Vision,* Kindle ed. Downers Grove: InterVarsity Press Academic. 2009.

_____. *Paul: In Fresh Perspective.* Minneapolis: Fortress Press, 2009.

Yadin, Yigael. *Masada: Herod's Fortress and the Zealot's Last Stand.* 1st ed. New York: Random House, 1966.

Yonge, C. D. *The Works of Philo: Every Good Man Is Free (Quod Omnis Probus Liber Sit),* Kindle ed. Peabody: Hendrickson Publishers, 2013.

_____. *The Works of Philo: On the Confusion of Tongues,* Kindle ed. Peabody: Hendrickson Publishers, 1991.

Yount, William R. *Created to Learn: A Christian Teacher's Introduction to Educational Psychology.* Nashville, Tennessee: Broadman & Holman Publishers, 1996.

Zahavy, Tzvee. *Kosher Talmud: Babylonian Talmud Hullin,* Kindle ed. Teaneck: Talmudic Books, 2012.

Zuck, Roy B. *Teaching as Jesus Taught.* Eugene, Oregon: Wipf & Stock Publishers, 2002.